them from synthetic, broken male culture into an authentic, powerful life in Christ."

—KENNY LUCK, president of Every Man Ministries, author of the God's Man Series, and men's pastor of Saddleback Church

"Troy Meeder nails it. *Average Joe* is a must-read for any guy who questions whether his life can make a difference in the world. Honest and straightforward, Troy reminds us that being 'average' does not equate with mediocrity and that with God nothing is impossible."

—ERIC CLOSE, actor, director, CBS

"Real heroes are desperately needed in our society today. Troy Meeder's book serves as an inspiration to any man who doubts his significance and desires to be a hero in God's eyes."

—RYAN DOBSON, author, speaker, and host of *Grounded Radio*

"An *excellent* read—like having a cup of 'joe' with your best friend and being infused with hope and destiny! I know it is time for 'iron to sharpen iron,' but this takes true courage. Troy Meeder dynamically opens this realm up in himself. Going through the study guide gave me the give and take I needed to feel as if Troy and I were truly looking into each other's heart. We men need to require more of ourselves, and this means we must take the chance and go deeper. After reading *Average Joe,* I face life with a new focus and purpose."

—RAFAEL OLGINE, average Joe and safety specialist

"This book is dynamite! If you are an average Joe, Troy will biblically blow up the lie that your existence and your life are not significant. And if you think you're not an average Joe, then you have an even deeper problem! Either way, this book is strong medicine that counters diseased thinking. The best men's book I've read in a long time."

—STEVE FARRAR, speaker, author of *Point Man*

AVERAGE JOE

God's Extraordinary Calling
to Ordinary Men

TROY MEEDER

MULTNOMAH
BOOKS

Average Joe
Published by Multnomah Books
12265 Oracle Boulevard, Suite 200
Colorado Springs, Colorado 80921

ISBN: 978-1-60142-307-8
ISBN: 978-1-60142-308-5 (electronic)

Cover design by Mark D. Ford

Published in association with the literary agency of Alive Communications
Inc., 7680 Goddard Street, Suite 200, Colorado Springs, CO 80920, www
.alivecommunications.com.

Published in the United States by WaterBrook Multnomah, an imprint of the
Crown Publishing Group, a division of Random House Inc., New York.

Multnomah and its mountain colophon are registered trademarks of Random
House Inc.

Library of Congress Cataloging-in-Publication Data
Meeder, Troy.
    Average Joe : God's extraordinary calling to ordinary men / Troy Meeder.
— 1st ed.
        p. cm.
    ISBN 978-1-60142-307-8 — ISBN 978-1-60142-308-5 (electronic) 1.
Christian men—Religious life. I. Title.
    BV4528.2.M44 2011
    248.8'42—dc22

                                    2010046630

Printed in the United States of America
2011—First Edition

10 9 8 7 6 5 4 3 2 1

For Kim.

For over three decades you have been at my side. We've climbed a hundred mountains, skied miles of back-country trails, played a thousand games of cribbage (I have lost most), and forged a life together. You are the love of my youth, the joy of my existence, and my very best friend. I can't imagine life without you.

CONTENTS

ACKNOWLEDGMENTS

For Toby: Your handshake is your bond. You're a man of few words, impeccable honesty, and a deep commitment to your family. You're the best of us average Joes.

For Goddy: We've labored together in the hot sun. You're the truest of friends. Thanks, mate.

For Worm: You're the example of what honor, integrity, and resolve should look like. You're the best of men. *Ooh Rah!*

For Hollywood: In an environment riddled with compromise, you remain a man of faith.

For Dad: You've taught me what it means to be a man. I love you.

For Kep: I will never forget fishing on Shasta Lake. "I wanna be like you."

For Bill: Thank you for loving my mom.

For Bruce: You've championed this project from the beginning. I thank you, my friend.

For my Jesus: You have rescued a sinful man. If there's anything good in me, it's because of Your saving grace, precious blood, and never-ending patience. I will love You forever.

The Average Joe

It's Monday.

The beginning of another week of...normalcy. Life as an average Joe is once again about to start its familiar grind.

If you are like me, we go through the same—often life-numbing—motions every day. We crawl out of bed at 0-dark-thirty to the sound of a screaming alarm clock, then stub our toe on our kid's "perfect" Christmas gift—the very one that last year cost us two days' pay! The dog needs to go outside. The kids are asleep but will definitely need some "dad time" later. The washer that sprang a leak still needs repair. The milk in the fridge is sour. The next-door neighbor parked his extra car in front of our driveway—again.

Oh, man, this is not the life you and I probably thought we would live!

As a boy I certainly had bigger plans than working in a cramped cubicle from eight to five, building widgets on the late shift at the local mill, or flipping burgers at the corner diner. My boyhood dreams never included a mortgage, diapers, traffic tickets, or cleaning out the gutters. Perhaps, like me, you dreamed of saving a life, flying a fighter jet, finding a cure for cancer, or even walking on the moon.

As boys, we had such high hopes to accomplish something great, to make a difference, to live a life that left a mark on those around us. We marveled at men like Chuck Yeager, Neil Armstrong, Buzz Aldrin, and the Reverend Billy Graham. We wanted to ride like John Wayne, lead like Ronald Reagan, drive like Mario Andretti, and win like the 1973 Miami Dolphins. All of us longed to be James Bond; instead we ended up looking and acting a bit like Archie Bunker.

Maybe you are asking the same question I ask: *What happened to my life?*

What happened for most of us is *reality*. Instead of finding fame and fortune, normalcy and "never enough" found us. We are average Joes, but is that really a problem? Definitely not! So-called average Joes are the ones who make the world work.

God seems to have a special fondness for average Joes. Before they accomplished extraordinary deeds, normal guys like Gideon, David, Peter, and Paul went about their farming, sheep herding, fishing, and tent making. Even Jesus, our Redeemer, Healer, and coming King, started out using a hammer and saw in a carpenter's shop.

You'll find average Joes are everywhere. Good men, honest men. They are hard working, genuine, and steadfast. More often than not, they are absent from the great halls of debate, the ivory towers of scholastic achievement, or the family trees of aristocracy. Instead they mow grass, sell insurance, build furniture, drive trucks, manage restaurants, and fix plumbing. They can be found serving coffee at the local diner, selling tires, or pastoring a small church. In our hurried pace we often pass them by as we rush off to our next appointment or event.

I suppose we might find an average Joe on Wall Street or in a government building in Washington DC, but if we did, he might be there only to fix, paint, or build something. Sometimes looked down upon, even dismissed as "less than," average Joes are the stable, dependable, resolute backbone of an ever-so-wavering society.

In a day when compromise and political correctness rule, these simple men—average Joes—seek truth and have an unshakable commitment to doing what is right. Ask them their opinion, and you will get an earful of resolute beliefs in God, country, and family. Strong in character, integrity, and principle, these are the unsung heroes of everyday life in America.

Average Joes Make a Difference

Being an average Joe is awesome, and I'm proud to call myself one. Too often, though, we average Joes feel ashamed of who we are. For some reason we don't seem to quite measure up. Why is that? What lies are we hearing and believing about our place in the world?

Many in contemporary society want to tell us our average Joe life is irrelevant, maybe even inconsequential. *What? Are you kidding me?* Tell that to the son who thinks his dad is the greatest. Tell that to the wife who has such deep respect and love for a husband who, day in and day out, goes to work at an unglamorous, demanding job to ensure his family is fed and sheltered. In fact, tell that to a savior named Jesus who chose twelve average Joes to help Him change the world.

Who cares if a man ever rafts the Colorado River, plays college football, or makes a million dollars before he's forty? That guy may never leave that cubicle he calls home forty-plus hours a week. He may always drive a minivan, sell appliances, and live in a suburban tract house. Is he any less a man?

No way.

Labeled "average," this Joe is that steadfast example of simple faith, honor, integrity, and character. He is the man who goes home at night to his wife and children. He mows the lawn, fixes the deck, reads to his kids, loves his wife, helps his friends, and serves his Lord. He's the kind of neighbor who will lend you his tools and watch your house when you're out of town. You trust him with your kids. He pays his bills and taxes. If he says he will be somewhere, he will be there—and on time. He's got his problems, and he owns them. Quite simply, average Joe is the very best of who we are.

This book is a challenge to look deep within yourself, to better understand the man God has made you to be, to find contentment in the life God has blessed you with. I will urge you to finally let go of boyish or unrealistic dreams and replace them with the wise passions, wisdom, and discipline of a man. It's time to make sure that integrity, honor, and moral steadfastness describe who you are.

Later in this book I will share some stories of average Joes that none of us will ever see on the front page or hear about on a cable news show. But in the world that really matters—God's kingdom—they are heroes of the faith, true examples of *how God uses ordinary men to change the world.*

Before we go on, I want to make something really clear: when I use the word *average,* I don't mean lazy, sloppy, inept, mediocre, or anything like that. A true average Joe works hard, give his all, makes a difference. And he does it without whining or feeling sorry for himself. An average Joe isn't expecting to get rich or famous. He's content knowing that the One whose opinion really counts is pleased with him.

While the world around us implies that we are nothing without fame, fortune, and recognition, we daily and without fanfare answer the call to perform the routine. As average Joes, we make a difference. The life we are living *does* have purpose, meaning, and honor.

Section One

WHEN WE WERE YOUNG

2

The Island

THE PLANE! THE PLANE!

In the late 1970s, millions of Americans gathered around their television set every Saturday night to watch a hit show on ABC. Tattoo, Mr. Roarke's faithful sidekick and assistant, would run up the circular stairs to ring the bell announcing the arrival of guests who'd paid fifty thousand dollars each to live out their dreams on a remote atoll in the Pacific called Fantasy Island. The stately Ricardo Montalban would gracefully greet each week's guests as they stepped out of the Grumman Widgeon seaplane onto the docks of their respective awaiting adventure. What would the plot be this week? Who would die? Who would survive? Who would live out their dreams in this perfect Eden? Who would not?

I still recall those late Saturday nights as a kid. My younger brother, Toby, and I would sprawl out with our pillows on the living room floor, popcorn in hand, to vicariously live the dreams of someone else through that innocuous television program. Every Saturday night our aspirations were played out on our antiquated television set in what someone had creatively described as "living color." For an hour we became professional football players, explorers, secret agents, and successful businessmen. While the characters in the show left the island with dreams sometimes fulfilled, sometimes not, we boys believed that our lives would play out just as we dreamed.

The enigmatic visions I saw in my sleep as a boy still retain their color, passion, and vividness forty years later. I can still recall many slumber adventures where I soared through cloudless skies in an F-4 Phantom. In those safe hours of rest, I was an Air Force pilot with stick in hand, rocketing through endless blue, experiencing the freedom and awesome responsibility of commanding the aircraft at my fingertips. There were no boundaries, no what-ifs, only the infinite passions of a young boy.

As happens with boys, the dream would instantly change course to some far-off galaxy of exploration. In my mind's eye I would see the men who traveled into space aboard the early Apollo missions. In explosions of light and fire, each Saturn rocket strained to escape the bonds of earth and reach into the cold, dark expanse of space. Would I, too, be one of them? Would I wear the patch of a mission commander on my shoulder?

The visions of young boys are as complex and changing as the tides. From pilot to deep-sea diver, fireman to explorer, astronaut to cowboy. Each night's sleep can bring a new frontier to explore.

Such were the hopes and passions of young boys growing up in the sixties and seventies. There were no limits. We lived in a world full of possibility, potential, and marvel. I wonder, did you dream that way? Are you, like me, an average Joe who lay awake at night hoping that one day he would accomplish the impossible, some improbable feat that Walter Cronkite would report on the *CBS Evening News*?

It doesn't matter what decades we grew up in, didn't we all have aspirations of a life filled with adventure and promise? Didn't we grow up optimistic that we would someday be president, a doctor, an explorer, or a professional athlete? Just like on *Fantasy Island,* we knew we would get off the plane, leave behind our boyish years, and step onto the deck of manhood ready to embrace the perfect adventure of our dreams.

The Race to Manhood

For some of us the journey to manhood began in the military. Others began their quest with marriage and children. My dream was to attend college—something my parents wanted for me too. But since they were hard-working folks trying to raise two sons and a daughter on blue-collar wages, any grand vision of a college degree meant I would have to pay for it myself.

After my June graduation from Enterprise High School in Redding, California, I worked tirelessly the entire summer to save money for college. Three months later, after seemingly round-the-clock work, I had just enough cash for the first two semesters.

I can still remember the day I left home, college bound. For years I had waited for this moment. With dreams piled as high as the junk in the backseat of my 1967 VW bug, I hugged my mom, shook my dad's hand, punched brother Toby in the arm, fired up the pathetic 60-hp motor of my V-dub, and roared away. The early morning sun was just cresting the tops of the old oak trees on the east side of our small acreage. With a cloud of dust roiling behind me, I made my way down our dirt drive and onto the small gravel country road in front of our place. My throat tightened as I was hit with the full understanding of the journey ahead: I was exchanging simple and safe childish dreams for new and uncertain realities. As I turned onto Interstate 5, with San Diego and Point Loma College a thirteen-hour drive away, I was confident that the next time I drove up that dusty dirt road to my childhood home, I would be on my way to becoming somebody.

My race from boyhood to manhood was on.

And I felt the energy, maybe something like a greyhound racing dog exploding from the gate at the sound of the bell. From a standstill, these incredible animal athletes accelerate to amazing speeds in a matter of seconds. Trained from birth and built for speed, the sleek, wiry greyhound is the fastest dog on the planet, reaching speeds of over forty miles per hour.

Circling an oval track, the greyhound charges hard after its quarry: a speeding mechanical hare. For its entire racing career, which may last for years, the greyhound focuses entirely on that furry prize. This dog will stress, strain, train, and sometimes risk life-altering injury in its single-minded quest to catch the ever-elusive, always-out-of-reach dummy hare. Nothing else seems to matter to the dog, just the prize.

While I am not a fan of this murky, sometimes troubling sport, I have seen videos of races run in the United States, the United Kingdom, and Australia. It is intriguing to watch the intense, extreme, never-compromising focus the greyhound has as it chases its target. As if its life depends on catching the fleeting quarry, the greyhound runs with complete abandonment. However, if the greyhound ever catches the fake hare, the game is over. The dog is ruined once it knows the prize is worthless. The only good option is for the dog to be retired, never to run again.

Although no metaphor is perfect, I see many similarities between greyhounds and countless men. As young boys we imagined what life would be like when we left the nest. We spent many a night lying awake, dreaming of the future we would embrace. For scores of us, those impressionable years were the staging ground for what was to come. We scrapped and fought for each opportunity to prepare for the race that would begin when we left home.

During the eons that preceded me and for as long as there's time, young men will leave the safety of what they knew as children and strike out on their own in hopes of making the grade, of being someone, of accomplishing the visions that invaded their sleep. We all burst from the gate with the intention of changing the world around us. Not unlike the greyhound leaping forward from its restraints, we see the prize before us: fame, fortune, happiness, and certain success waiting just around the corner.

WHAT HAPPENED TO OUR DREAMS?

I left for college in 1978. Now that there are probably fewer years ahead than there are behind me, I reflect on the race I have run. In looking back to those incredible early days, I realize there was nothing average about the dreams and plans I had for myself. Do you feel the same? As you were crossing the threshold from boy to man, did you dream of faraway places, powerful accomplishments, life-changing events, of living a life that far exceeded "the average"? Like the greyhound, did you race off from boyhood and run hard to catch the prize? As the perceived shackles of youth fell away, did you, like me, burst forward in hopes of doing the exceptional?

As I consider my life, I left the gate just like the guy next to me. I worked hard, trained, planned, dreamed. Yet for some reason my life—and your life—turned out different from what we anticipated. We've given it all we have, only to seemingly fall short.

Why is it that some men seem to achieve everything and the rest of us do not? Did we lose the race? Or is there more to the story?

Each episode of *Fantasy Island* ended with the visitors going back home to the life they'd left behind. With memories packed away like the clothing in their luggage, they made their way to the dock. Some left with dreams fulfilled; some did not. Sounds like real life, doesn't it?

Some of us have lived the dreams and fantasies we envisioned as boys. We have reached the pinnacle of success, climbed mountains, soared to the heavens—all the while laughing as each dream was fulfilled. Most of us have not. *We are the ones on the dock in* Fantasy Island *at the end of the show, standing with luggage in hand, wondering what the heck happened to our dream…to our* life.

All four gospels of the New Testament record the denial of Jesus by Peter. For months Peter had traveled with the Messiah. He had eaten, walked, talked, laughed, and cried with the King of kings. Peter was now a disciple of the Messiah. Prior to meeting Jesus, Peter had been a fisherman. Day after day his life had centered on the mundane, dirty, smelly job of fishing. Outside of his family and friends, no one knew or cared what Peter did. He was just another fisherman making a living on the Sea of Galilee.

But now Peter had become something more than a fisherman; he was somebody—a disciple of Jesus, a chosen one. What were his dreams? In his sleep did he see himself one day sitting at the right hand of Jesus in a glorious kingdom? Was he a bigwig in the court of the King? I know that if I had been in Peter's shoes, I would have had visions of grandeur. Given the opportunity to hang out with the King, I would have become arrogant, prideful, and self-centered.

And then, in an instant, Peter's life went from that perfect picture of the dream to a pile of broken glass: he denied the King of kings. *What now, Peter? Back to the boat and an anonymous life with the fishnets?*

With the crowing of the rooster, Peter's dreams were seemingly lost. Even though Jesus looked at Peter with eyes filled with love, the man Jesus had called "the rock" could only weep bitterly as his dreams died.

As you contemplate these words, do you understand Peter's tears? As you recall the dreams of boyhood, the passions of youth, even the hopes of innocence, do you see failure rearing its hideous head?

Have your boyhood dreams shattered like broken glass at your feet? Did you once think you would be somebody that you're not, only to end up average? Just another average Joe?

How in the world did this happen?

3

The Hole

A day in my life...

How did it come to this? The walls of my self-dug mud prison are crumbling all around me. What started as a simple excavation project has turned into a five-foot-deep hole that's now filling with human waste.

Standing knee-deep in muck pouring from a broken sewer line, I struggle to comprehend how I had possibly come to this place. I mean, come on, God... I gave it all up to serve You...to serve kids. I mean, I could have been somebody. Now this!

There has to be some place in Scripture that says that when you give up a career in corporate America and choose to become a junior high youth pastor, with all its amazing "benefits" (such as low pay, long hours, and dealing with...well...junior high kids), shouldn't there be special consideration for...me? There must be a verse in Scripture that promises that such a sacrifice will bring great rewards, not only in heaven, but...here?

Okay, maybe not written in those exact words, but at least a paraphrase. I mean, come on, God! A little help down here!

◦◦◦

As a young man, I served for fourteen years as both a volunteer and salaried staff member at a large church in central Oregon. While this was no megachurch, it was the largest body of believers east of the Cascade Mountains in Oregon. Westside Church is an incredible place, led by pastor Ken Johnson, a man I deeply respect and call a friend. I came to Westside in 1983 as a volunteer for the then-small high school youth program. For eight years my wife, Kim, and I served as best we knew how. Youth pastors came and went, some on good terms, others not. I began to see how important words like *honesty, integrity, character,* and *strong moral compass* were to describe a good pastor as well as a good man. How God delights in not what a man knows, his stature, or his ability to lead the masses. He is more interested in who the man is.

Serving at Westside as a volunteer was one of the greatest times of learning and growth in my life. And while I loved sharing in the lives of kids and shouldering the ministry with the paid staff, I always longed to be on staff, to be one of the pastoral team. *To be somebody.*

My chance came in the fall of 1991. I gave up a promising career in human resources to *finally* be somebody. On October 1, I hung up the clothes of an average Joe and donned my superhero cape as *junior high youth pastor* of Westside Church! From now on I would make a difference in lives. In my young, immature mind, I was convinced that the title meant you were something. I believed that if I could have *pastor* in front of my name, then I had purpose, meaning, and a life fulfilled. My mailbox started receiving letters that were

addressed to the Reverend *Kenneth Troy Meeder*. Hot dog! *Okay...
You and me, God...we are going to build the biggest, coolest, most awesome youth ministry in the Pacific Northwest.*

The hole continues to fill. Human waste is now knee
high. I can't get out! The slippery walls of my self-dug
crater won't allow a foothold. Really. I am going to
drown in...

Snow starts to fall, not the fluffy, dry stuff we
dream of as a child. No. This is the cold, wet, bone-
chilling kind of snow that, when the flakes hit the
ground, turn everything into a muddy, brown, slippery
slush. The stinking soup is rising. Human feces,
tissue, unmentionables all float by as the broken
sewer line spews its filthy contents. I feel panic. Mud
and rocks from the sides of my hole are caving in on
me. Jesus, how did it come to this? What did I ever
do but serve You? And now this!

For six years I had the life-changing, incredible pleasure of serving on
the pastoral staff at Westside. While I was originally hired to pastor
the junior high students, in time my responsibilities included the
college and career group and eventually the senior high ministry.
Life was good. I was given a nice corner office with a secretary and a
generous monthly budget. The church built a tremendous new
youth center. Every Tuesday night we rocked the building with a

band, food, and 250 to 300 students. Maximum Security Company was known as *the* place to be east of the Cascades. I couldn't have dreamed it up any better than it was. Gone were the days of being just Troy. I was now that guy who ran the biggest youth ministry in central Oregon. My identity had changed. I was *the man.*

It was a rainy Wednesday afternoon when Doug, my overseer, called me into his office. "We are concerned that you may be losing your passion for kids," he nervously shared with me. "Ken and I have been having some long conversations about your future here at the church. While there is no obvious reason we can see to ask you to step down, Pastor Ken feels that God is calling you elsewhere and that September 30 is to be your last day."

"What? *Are you kidding me? What have you and Ken been smoking? This ministry is the biggest and the best in the area. Lives are being changed. Kids are getting saved.* Are you crazy?"

Pride and arrogance began to rear their ugly heads. I had become what I hated. Yes…I was no longer an average Joe. I had the title. In my own stupid little brain, I thought I was *someone.* I was convinced that *I* was the reason the ministry was succeeding. I knew that if I left, everything would change. I even prayed that Ken and Doug would live to regret their "shallow, shortsighted decision." In wanting to be *someone,* I had become what I hated—an arrogant, self-centered, pigheaded jerk.

Six weeks later, on September 30, I walked off the campus of Westside Church with backpack in hand. There was no fanfare. The church didn't split. There were tears from a few, and some parents of teenagers were upset. But the place didn't fall into a deep chasm because I was gone. The youth ministry moved forward without me. I wondered if this was how Moses felt when he left Egypt. He was the man! All Egypt knew him. He was an heir to Pharaoh's kingdom. He was a *somebody.* I was a *somebody.* Not anymore.

SHAPED THROUGH ADVERSITY

The clay was beginning to get ready for the Master's hands.

I needed a job, so I took a position as a landscaper and worked for an incredible man of faith named Frank, who knew I needed some help. While there was little room for another man on his construction team, Frank offered me a chance to make a few bucks as his landscape supervisor—a fancy title for the guy who gets to dig trenches, plant trees, trim shrubs, and, yes, fix broken sewer lines. That's why I was in the hole on October 4…

I try time and time again to claw my way out of the crumbling trench I have dug. The sewer line continues its insidious release of putrid, filthy human waste. Now up to my waist, the muck is threatening to drag me under.

So this is it, I think. This is the testament of my life? This is where the dreams and plans end up?

From my pit I curse God. I yell at the One who created me, "How could You do this to me? I served You with my whole heart. I gave up everything to become a pastor, a man who served You. What am I to do now? You have ruined me. You have abandoned me!"

I wonder how many of us average Joes have felt that way. We seek to find fulfillment in lives of importance, prestige, and position. We spend our precious days clawing for the next rung on the ladder. We will not rest until we are the boss or get an office with our name on the door. We sometimes compromise integrity, honor, and character in search of wealth, fame, and recognition. We would sell our soul to be the king of the castle. It's only later when our kingdom falls apart that we cry out to God, asking why He would abandon us.

He never does, of course. It is in times such as these that we truly see who He is.

I try one more time to climb out. Miraculously, I find a foothold that I am certain was not there before. With one quick lunge up and out, I escape the quickly filling pit I had dug for myself. I yell to a friend a few hundred yards away, and he quickly shuts down the line that feeds the break I had created.

The flowing sewer stops.

At the edge of my hole, I lie, shivering from the cold sleet that now has soaked me to the bone. The stench makes me nauseous. I know I am a pitiful sight, but I am alive!

I wonder if, in that moment, the Creator was looking down with a gentle, maybe even sad smile. I wonder if in His heart He knew this was exactly what I needed to refine me. Was it in that hole that the much-needed death of the pious, self-centered man I was began? Was it there that God began the process of turning arrogance into modesty, pride into humility, and resistance to submission? Possibly even weakness into strength.

I believe that healing in my life began that very day.

I am thankful that the love the Father has for us trumps the compassion He must feel as He breaks, refines, and molds the men He can use for His purposes. As Creator, He must find it difficult to cause heartache in His creation. Like a dad, He allowed the breaking to occur in my life and, I believe, grieved. Yet a good father knows that more often than not, pain, sorrow, and struggle are exactly what's needed to refine the heart of a boy…a man…an average Joe.

TRUE CONTENTMENT

In that hole is where my life change began. A. W. Tozer wrote, "Whom God would use greatly, He will hurt deeply." The process of hurting had finally begun in my life. I had wasted years in seeking recognition and acknowledgment. I had wanted to be somebody, but there is no need to strive to be anything more than a servant of our Creator. We expend ourselves, our precious life, and our very existence in the pursuit of significance, prestige, wealth, and fame. I believe that these pursuits are meaningless, never ending, and often offer only hollowness, hunger, and pain. We seek to be something our Creator never intended us to be: self-important, shortsighted, and earthly minded.

I believe that every man—yes, even an average Joe—can and will be used greatly by God if he allows himself to be broken, refined, and shaped more into His image.

Could I ask you something? Are you in a hole today? Has the pursuit of whatever is outside of God's perfect plan skewed your understanding of what it means to be a man of faith, honor, and integrity? Has the pursuit of a dream been the very trap that has sunk you in a foul hole? I'm here to say it: You will never find true contentment in the pursuit of the next rung on the corporate ladder, the faster car, the more expensive vacation, or the extreme man adventure. While all those things are awesome and potentially life changing, they are not what your soul longs after.

Peace, contentment, and honor are to be found in the simple.

All of us have spent time in *the hole.* We average Joes know all too well the potentially life-crippling sorrow of seeking what we think will bring happiness, only to realize it can never be found. Life doesn't have to be that way: Jesus Christ died to give us life. But what does that life need to look like for us to feel complete, sufficient, and necessary?

After spending years searching for grandeur, I can tell you with certainty that real joy, fulfillment, and life lie in the quiet of an early morning sunrise, the laughter of children, the soft whisper from a wife—even in something as simple as a hot cup of coffee in front of a wood stove on a cold winter's morning. Those are the moments that make life full and rich.

Outside of a life in service to those around us and to our Creator, there is no life. You will never find true purpose, true peace, or true fulfillment outside a life lived in the shadow of the King.

It took time in *the hole* for me to embrace contentment in the average.

I don't know what your life experiences have been. I don't know your specific dreams, failures, and setbacks. But I do know that the Lord of all is with you. His perfect plan is being lived out in you.

Will you trust Him for the future that lies just ahead?

As you read on, I want to introduce you to some average Joes. These are men who have changed the world around them. Some of these guys have made a huge impact on many lives; most have not. They are ordinary men who through disappointment, struggle, and mind-numbing boredom have survived the holes and exchanged disappointment, struggle, and monotony for exhilaration, integrity, and passion.

It's a very good thing, really, to be an average Joe.

Section Two

GUTS, GRIT, AND SAND

4

The Gardener

AVERAGE JOES ARE EVERYWHERE. Good men, honest men. They are hard working, genuine, and steadfast. Often they are found doing the mundane...even mowing the grass at a Southern California university.

I met Jim in 1978 during the second week of my freshman year at Point Loma College (PLC). Beneath a warm sun, Southern California was relaxing in the beauty of an early fall day on the coast. From my dorm room window on the third floor of Young Hall, I saw the Pacific Ocean spread out before me like a soft blue blanket. The surf was gentle, only three- to four-foot swells quietly rolling ashore.

I had arrived from Redding as one of hundreds of freshmen who all stuck out like neon signs on campus. We were always lost, always late for class, always a little nervous, and probably a bit homesick. Crawling out of bed that morning, I was keenly aware that my life would forever be changed by just being here. This was not the quiet back country of my family's small neighborhood. San Diego in the 1970s was idyllic—perfect weather, clean air, and warm sunshine abounded. Point Loma College was then a relatively small Nazarene university bursting at the seams with students bound for a myriad of professions. All around me walked future doctors, lawyers, pastors, and scientists.

Candidly, as I made my way around the campus, I wondered who I was to be in such an incredible place. My family wasn't wealthy. My dad was an average Joe who worked tirelessly in a small country market down the road from our modest house. My mom labored just as hard raising two boys and my baby sister while holding down a job as a hairdresser. My parents had dreamed of sending a son or daughter to college, but financially it wasn't in the cards. My path to PLC was paved by months of hard work, saving tips, and student loans. Yet here I was. I had made it.

Leaving Young Hall that warm sunny morning, I felt larger than life. I was on my own. My dream of going to college had come true.

The first time I saw Jim, he was whistling as he drove an old, rusting riding lawn mower, grooming the grass that surrounded the cafeteria. With surgical precision Jim made each run back and forth across the lawn. The newly cut grass resembled the intricate patterns at Candlestick Park just before game time. Looking to be in his sixties, Jim clothed his medium-sized frame in an ancient pair of Carhartt coveralls. He wore a classic John Deere hat, and his eyes twinkled through thick lenses set in large, Phyllis Diller–style frames. What a picture!

I have to be honest—I was in a hurry that day. Like most freshmen, I was late to a class that I was having a tough time finding. But when I glanced at Jim, he gave me a broad, infectious smile. Stopping his motorized chariot, Jim raised his callused hand in a friendly wave. Little did I know that his smile, gentle demeanor, and welcoming gesture were the beginning of a friendship that would root down-to-earth wisdom deep within me. We exchanged a handshake and a few words of greeting. He warmly reached out to a homesick country boy—who reached back.

A few days later, because my finances were tight, Jim offered me a job as a landscaper on the campus. As the head groundskeeper, he could hire some extra hands for the school year, and I was one of the lucky ones he chose. Over the next nine months, Jim and I were to spend many hours fixing lawn mowers, sharpening shears, weeding flower gardens, and of course, mowing grass.

Showing up for work my first day, I was certain I would dazzle my new employer with all my homegrown wisdom and skill. I was "experienced," having mowed grass, weeded, planted, and even trimmed a few trees while growing up. Boy, was I wrong! To me, mowing grass was a chore; to Jim, it was an art.

"Each blade of grass is part of a small clump," he said. "Each clump is a part of the whole. The entire lawn before you is thousands, if not millions, of tiny plants, all woven together in a wonderful tapestry of life."

"What! Are you kidding me? It's just grass," I answered. My boyish response was a bit condescending. Jim smiled and proceeded to tell me how, like the grass, we believers are all woven together in a living expression of our Maker. "It's a beautiful picture of creation."

I listened. I could tell already that Jim was a unique person.

Jim went on and told me that he was charged with making sure that the grass he mowed would look just right to his Creator. That Jesus, the Lord of his life, would see Jim's love for Christ in the way he carefully mowed grass. That each pass with the mower would be seamed with the next. That the corners and edges would be trimmed just right as to not show any stress to the grass. That he made sure the blades on the mower were sharp so that each time the blade met the grass, the cut would be clean, not ragged.

Jim led me to a recently mowed area beside the biology lab. With an impish grin he asked, "Does this grass look okay?"

"Sure," I responded.

"Look closer."

"Well, the grass looks a bit off color, maybe a bit stressed, like it isn't getting enough water," I said.

After I stated that mild observation, Jim asked me to sit with him by an ancient shade tree, where he shared the first of many simple but incredible lessons in life. Here's the essence of what Jim told me that morning: Not unlike the grass, we as believers are all woven together in a beautiful tapestry that carries the blood thread of Jesus Christ. The grass grows. So does the believer. Life has a tendency to beat us up a bit, just like the grass. Every day people come by and walk on the grass; they spill Cokes and food; they mash the grass down. In our life, Satan, that thief and liar, is the worst. He shows up with his worn-out lies and tricks, just like a mower with dull, worn-out blades, and chops us off.

The off color I'd noticed that day was, according to Jim, a result of thousands of little blades of grass that were ripped and torn instead of cleanly mowed. Each blade of grass, when closely examined, had a small tear or rip that revealed a brown edge. To the untrained eye, the grass just looked dry; to Jim it looked broken and worn.

As believers we go through life with the bumps and bruises we each feel when we are stepped on, trampled a bit, or dumped on. That affects us personally. When the enemy runs us over as a corporate body of believers, the world sees the whole tapestry as broken and battered. Then, just like my friend Jim with his lawn mower, Jesus comes along and prunes and trims us. Not with an unsharpened, worn-out blade like our enemy's, but with the razor-sharp edge of His Word, will, and love.

Jim fired up the old John Deere mower that day, and after he made one pass, the result was magical: the once-ragged and discolored grass was now a crisp, beautiful green. With each pass I saw the change. The browning mass transformed before my eyes. The sharp blades of Jim's favorite mower trimmed the living carpet just enough—not so much as to damage the living plant but enough to lift each blade of grass and remove the ragged brown edge, leaving it fresh and new.

PRUNED BY THE MASTER GARDENER

Isn't that like Jesus? We are sinful, selfish, self-centered beings in need of pruning. "Hey man, I'm good. I don't need any help from this Jesus character. Just look at old Ed down the road. He goes to bars, cheats on his wife, and is never home with his kids. I am *twice* the man he is!"

Are you? Am I? When Jesus comes to prune, we feel like we are being picked on, worked over, or hurt. Yet when the Master finishes, we are left standing a bit taller, our sinful edges pruned, the true color of who He made us to be shining through. We find ourselves ready for life.

Walking across campus to my dorm room that evening, I was struck with the realization that, while trimming is painful at times, our Savior desperately wants to remove the worn, broken, and tattered parts of our lives. We all have so much in us that is ugly, damaged, or crushed, and we are so sure that no one will notice that we look just like everyone else. We think that we have it all so together. I wonder, though, what the world sees when it looks across our church, our workplace, our home. Does it see brokenness, a life of ragged compromise, maybe even sin disguised as a bit of dry, brown discoloration?

As I crawled into bed that night, because of an average Joe like Jim, I found myself asking questions that I never thought I would ask: *What needs to be trimmed in me? Am I ragged, broken, battered? How does the world see me?*

As I lay in my bunk, I realized that Satan had left a broken, battered path across my heart. The short years of my young life had indeed left me in need of a trimming by my Savior. In the quiet moments before sleep, I prayed that Jesus would begin to prune out the old, rotting stuff in my life. I wanted to change. Even if it would be painful, I wanted Him to move across my heart and cut away the dead leftovers of a life of sin.

And as only Jesus can, He did.

For nine months I enjoyed the strong embrace of Jim's wisdom, care, and compassion. We talked about many things: how seedlings become plants and how the Creator packed all the DNA information of a huge shade tree into something as small as an acorn. Jim laughed about this and said, "If God can create a huge tree out of an acorn, just imagine what he can and will do through you?" His eyes twinkled as he looked at me. In that instant, I felt like I could accomplish anything. I realized that if God cared so much for the result of the life of an acorn, how much more was He concerned with me.

How could such a man, a gardener, an average Joe make so much sense? We read books written by great leaders, we marvel at the accomplishments of superstars, we stand in awe of those who make headlines. Yet here I was being tutored by a simple man of simple means. In the eyes of the world, Jim was a blue-collar, uneducated, worn-out old man who had little value in the so-called big scheme of things. He was just an average Joe living an average life. But what a difference he made in the world around him!

Jim loved the earth. For hours he and I cultivated the black soil around campus. Gently he would add peat moss and manure to hard, used-up ground. He cared so much for dirt that had far outlived its usefulness. He once spoke of what a jokester our God is that only He can make soil usable again by adding manure to it. I can still recall Jim laughingly sharing how it is the manure in our life that creates the "garden" for us to grow in. Scripture confirms that "God turned into good what you meant for evil" (Genesis 50:20).

We moan and groan that our lives are so tough. We cry out to

God, asking why He is allowing such turmoil and difficulty. But like Jim cultivating the old, hard, dry soil, so Jesus does with us. Especially us guys. We get so wrapped up in what's right in front of our faces that we forget Jesus is at work in our hearts. Or at least He is trying to break up the crusty ground of our lives in order for the seeds of His truth, patience, and wisdom to grow.

I know I can be so pigheaded that I miss potentially life-changing instruction from the King. It truly is the manure or desert experiences that can be the best tools Jesus uses to break up our brittle, dry, rocky ground.

This is what happened to Moses. Banished from his home in Egypt, Moses spent years roaming the desert. A man of great intellect, promise, and a certain future as royalty, Moses was taken from his home by a God who loved him enough to spend forty years breaking up the hard soil of his heart.

The book of Exodus records Moses fleeing an angry pharaoh. From pharaoh's palace, Moses escaped to the land of Midian where "years passed" (Exodus 2:23). Moses, the adopted son of a king, was reduced to a shepherd, an average Joe, chasing sheep in the wasteland of Midian. There, in the sands and heat of the desert, God restored the soil in Moses enough to create a man worthy to lead the exodus of God's chosen people.

FIND A "JIM"

My final memory of Jim is on a sunny, warm Thursday, May 17, 1979. Our small team of student landscapers had decided to meet in Jim's shop for a final get-together. We laughed and joked about all that had happened over the past nine months. Stories of flat tires, runaway tractors, mole hunting, and exploding Weed Eaters kept us laughing until our sides hurt. We drank soda pop, ate a cake baked by the cafeteria staff, and reveled in the joy of the moment.

As the afternoon waned, one by one the guys I'd worked with made their way back to the dorm. I chose to stay until the last. As Jim and I were cleaning up the bits of cake, empty cups, and plates, I heard the seriousness in Jim's voice. "God has plans for you, Troy," he said quietly. "I am not a prophet, only a gardener, but I sense deeply that Jesus has a simple but important life set aside for you." Youthful curiosity demanded that I give Jim my full attention as he spoke: "You will be a man of the earth. Your life will not be the same as those around you. You are a cultivator. You will be instrumental in seeing things grow. Your hands are made for the soil, both in an earthly sense as well as in kingdom building."

Jim's gentle, ancient eyes glassed over as he reached out his weathered hand. "Let your yes be yes and your no be no. Never compromise your integrity, and let your handshake be your bond."

Through my own watery eyes, I thanked this incredible man for sharing life with me. As I left the shop, Jim—as he always did when closing up for the day—loudly hummed some old gospel tune while closing up his antique Stanley lunchbox, turning off the lights, and locking the door.

My last pictured memory of Jim is of him walking across the rich green grass he had groomed that day. In a perfect "Jim moment," he stopped to pull a weed, pick up a piece of trash, and smooth the bark mulch in one final flower bed so that it was just right.

That evening I wrote this in my journal:

I worked my final day with Jim. While I am looking forward to getting home, I am a bit sad that I am fairly certain I will not be returning to PLC. The funds have run out, my grades are not that great, and I feel strongly that God has different plans for me. I will miss Jim. His wisdom, kindness, and gentle good humor have become very familiar to me. I find myself at peace when we are working together.

He is an extraordinary man. I have learned so much over these past nine months: how to properly groom the grass, the value of manure, the wonder of creation, the beauty of the Creator in His creation, and of course, how to just be quiet and listen to the world. I think most of all I take with me a tiny portion of the wisdom of a gentle, kind man named Jim. I can only hope that I will become a man like him. A man of steadfast commitment, simple wisdom, and unwavering truth.

A man can search the world over and never once meet a person like Jim. Yes, in the eyes of the world, Jim was an old, uneducated man who walked a bit crookedly and was not very appealing to look at. In my eyes, and more importantly, in the eyes and heart of his Savior, Jim was a giant. This average Joe solidified standards in my life that I have never forgotten:

- Let your yes be yes and your no be no.
- Your handshake is your bond.
- The body of Christ is a tapestry of living creatures all joined together by the blood thread of Jesus.
- Everyone needs a little manure in his or her life sometimes.

Looking back over the past thirty-plus years, I am amazed by how Jim's simple words have forever changed my life—words spoken by an average Joe who I never would have known if I hadn't slowed down for a moment and smiled at an old man mowing grass with a rusty John Deere tractor.

There are Jims all around us. They work in the shadows of our everyday lives.

Find them.

5

The Mark

"You need to come to California right away. Your grand-father is dying."

The words struck my heart like a hammer blow. My aunt Dolores was in tears as she shared the tragic news that my sole remaining grandparent, the patriarch of the Meeder family, was suffering from bone cancer. She wept as she described the terrifying and rapid decline the insidious disease had wrought on Grandpa's body. "He is not the man you knew as a boy," she sadly reported. "The cancer has stolen the man we all knew. Please come down as soon as you can."

I didn't need to think about it; I had to go.

Kim, with wonderful compassion, smiled as she hugged and kissed me good-bye. "Cherish each moment you have with Grandpa. These may be your last," she said with tearful eyes as I climbed inside my old Dodge pickup truck.

Rolling down our gravel drive, I thought about how time is a thief that never sleeps and stalks all of us like a predator. Now, sadly, my friend, my grandpa was succumbing to the thief. Time was ticking away.

The trip to Redding from Bend is a fairly simple, straight-forward, five-hour drive south along Highway 97. The small two-lane highway cuts through forests of Douglas fir, lodge pole pine, and aspen. To the west the skyline reaches to the heavens as Mount Bachelor, Mount Scott, Mount Thielsen, Mount McGloughlin, and the majestic Mount Shasta pass by your window. Along this corridor it's not uncommon to see mule deer, coyote, elk, and an occasional bald eagle soaring over Klamath Lake.

I usually enjoyed this drive, but not today. I found it hard to keep from speeding. "Lord, please watch over this crazy fool as he drives way too fast," I prayed. As I drove through Klamath Falls, I passed an older couple pulling a faded fishing boat behind their Chevy pickup truck. By the looks of the boat's rigging, I concluded they were headed to the coast to do some salmon fishing. Grandpa had been a commercial fisherman, and salmon were always his favorite. Tears filled my eyes, and I struggled to keep the truck on the road.

Childhood memories flooded my thoughts...

Some thirty-five years ago, on a hot, summer Thursday, Dad, Toby, and I took the winding highway out of Redding west to the small coastal town of Trinidad, California. What a relief it would be to exchange the sweltering valley heat of Redding for the cool breeze of the California coast. We were going salmon fishing with Grandpa. We had four short days, just enough time, if we were lucky, to catch plenty of fish.

Grandpa loved summers fishing in the cold currents of the Pacific Ocean along the northern California coastline. He would pack up his boat with a ton of supplies, and he and Grandma would head west to enjoy June and July on the coast. As a retired butcher, Grandpa was an average Joe. Small in stature, Irish and German by blood, he was a firecracker of a man who loved fishing, telling stories, and sipping Crown Royal whiskey. Grandpa was not an alcoholic; he just never missed a chance to "live a little." I still remember how dinners with Grandpa always meant steak, fried potatoes, and "a snort." Vegetables and salads were rare; T-bones were not.

At five feet eight inches, my grandpa was a joke-cracking, TV-wrestling-watching, leather-handed man who said what he meant and meant what he said. He never backed down, always had a smile, never missed a chance to fish, and dearly loved my mom. She and I still share stories of how he would turn tragedy into laughter. When life would get her down, Mom could always find solace in the company of this tough but exceedingly gentle man.

It's a four-hour drive from Redding to Trinidad. As a kid, I swore it took days to get there. My brother and I pestered Dad with the classic questions: "Are we there yet? Are you sure we have enough gas? Can we stop for something to eat? I'm hungry! Dad, can we stop at the next bathroom?" These universal petitions of kids everywhere must be the proverbial burr in the saddle for parents. My dad is a patient man, but I am sure there were times when he wanted to stuff socks in our mouths.

On arrival, we always found Grandpa at his campsite, fixing the fishing poles, fussing with the nineteen-foot boat, or if we arrived late in the day, sitting in a lawn chair and enjoying a Crown. This Thursday, when we pulled into Trinidad late in the afternoon, Grandpa was in his usual animated mood. He had chosen to dock his boat at a slip in the harbor where it was rigged and waiting for us.

Like so many of our previous fishing adventures, that evening was a blast. It was guy time—no girls allowed. We ate steak, played cards, and laughed late into the night. Of course, "late" for Grandpa and our dad was 8:30 or 9:00 p.m. Dad would always raise his hands into the air and then slap his lap, exclaiming, "That's enough for me, boys! The old man's going to hit the hay." Toby and I knew that was the signal for bed. Sleep escaped me that night. It was then, and still is now, hard for me to sleep the night before an adventure...

THE CALM BEFORE...

"Come on, boys. It's time to get up. You guys going to sleep all day?" Grandpa asked with a laugh. Through sleepy eyes, I looked outside and saw only stars. "Come on, Grandpa. It's like midnight or something."

"Boys, it's 4 a.m. and the fish are waiting!"

Yeah, right, I thought. *The fish are waiting. Ha! They're probably still asleep too.*

The Trinidad harbor had a small diner where the local fishermen gathered every morning to fuel up for the day ahead. It was a place where everyone knew everyone else. Waitresses at this antiquated cafe had worked there not for months but years, even decades. The owner was the cook, the one who slung plates loaded with sausage and eggs, pancakes spilling over the edge, chicken-fried steak with stick-to-your-ribs gravy, waffles with real maple syrup, mason jars filled with orange juice or whole milk, steaming mugs of hot coffee, and—my personal favorite—slabs of greasy bacon and fried eggs. That Friday morning was no different. Toby and I stuffed ourselves with farm-fresh eggs, hash browns, thick peppered bacon, homemade biscuits, and cups of hot black coffee. We were salmon fishermen, after all, and by golly, at the ripe old ages of fourteen and eight, we weren't going to let anyone outeat us. Our motto was "If you're going to go...go big!"

A brief aside: In an era of fat-free egg substitutes, granola, fake butter, and chai tea, does anyone truly enjoy eating anymore? Women, if you are reading this, may I offer a peek into the inner sanctum of a man? While I would be the first to say that we all need to make sure we do our best to eat healthy, take our vitamins, exercise, and all the rest of that pain-in-the-backside stuff, there are times when your guy needs to sit down and wrap himself around the biggest bacon-mushroom-onion cheeseburger he can hold or dive into a humongous plate of sausage, eggs, hash browns, gravy, and a big ol' fat biscuit smothered in real butter and homemade jam. Trust me, for a guy, this is living!

Back to the story…

Of course, later in the day, Grandpa and Dad would always get a real kick out of watching Toby and me lose our prized go-big breakfast over the side of our rising and falling fishing boat from hell! Bacon and eggs never tasted that good the second time around.

With bait boxes full of frozen anchovies, hot coffee in our thermos, and the sun rising to steal the day from the clutches of night, Grandpa slowly eased his boat out of Trinidad Harbor. I was always amazed how he could point to some unseen location, miles from shore, and growl, "That's where the fish are today, boys." How did he know that? We had no GPS in those days, no cell phones with tracking beacons. We did have a crude floating compass that would roll with the waves. In essence it was a ball set in liquid that reset itself as the boat tossed about, but there was no land in sight that we could use for bearings. Between us and Japan or Russia there were only millions of square miles of open ocean. Yet chewing on his customary unlit cigar, with a mug of hot cream of mushroom soup in hand, he would point out to sea and throttle up Big John, which is what he called the 125-horsepower outboard on his boat, and away we would go. This day was no different.

For an hour we chugged along on a northwesterly 320-degree heading to a seamount fifteen miles from shore where Grandpa had heard all the fish were gathering. The ocean was calm and flat. Seabirds of all types trailed along.

When we arrived at the spot, the routine was simple and predictable: bait up and get it wet. We set our bait, weight, and depth and commenced to getting on with the chore at hand—fishing. Trying to impress him with my fourteen-year-old wisdom, I told Toby that this was as good as it gets.

For several hours we laughed, caught fish, told lies, and just enjoyed being alive. I still remember my dear, sensitive grandpa saying, while Toby and I once again lost our "go big" breakfast into the Pacific, "You boys want some jack cheese and a cup of mushroom soup?" What a comedian. My face was as green as the ocean! Somehow soup and cheese didn't seem like the best idea.

The Pacific Ocean, vast and teeming with life, was beautiful that day—an incredible work of our Creator. For hours we enjoyed the company of a warm sun and calm seas. But that was about to change. Late in the afternoon Mother Nature decided it was time to alter the rules of the game. Dad noticed it first: way off to the west, an ominous squall line was replacing the blue sky.

...THE STORM

We had a choice: keep on fishing or head for cover. At times like this, decisions guided by the wisdom of gray hair far outweigh any youthful desire to buck the odds. With clarity born from years at sea, Grandpa gave the order: "Time to go, boys. The ocean has changed her mind, and we are not going to challenge her." Fishing lines were reeled in, bait boxes stored, coats donned, and Big John fired up. We headed for home.

To this day I am still in awe of how fickle nature can be. In the minutes it took for us to set the boat up for the trip home, the weather changed dramatically. For hours the Pacific had been graceful, but now driving wind and rain replaced the clear blue sky. The sea turned from a quiet jade green to an angry, ominous gray. We had rocked in fairly gentle three- to four-foot seas all day, but now our small fishing boat rose and fell with ten- to twelve-footers. When the boat crested a wave, we could see several hundred yards, but when we sank to the bottom of the trough, all we saw was furious water and a gray sky.

We were in trouble.

At times like these, powerful, lifelong memories are cast in stone, never to be forgotten. As though it happened yesterday, I can see my steel-eyed grandpa, face to the wind, hat pulled down tight, cigar clenched, his five-foot-something body rigid as he steered our boat toward home. *But which way was home?* This was 1974, and we had only a coastal map and a crude compass that was almost impossible to read as the boat plunged up and down. I had *no* idea which way was land. The cloud bank had completely surrounded us. We were fifteen miles out at sea, bobbing like a cork in a bathtub. I thought for sure this was my last day alive and that months later some Japanese fishing trawler would find what was left of our boat drifting in the North Pacific.

Boy, was I wrong.

I was not taking into account that I was fishing with my granddad. I had forgotten that while I had no clue about how to get home, he did. Grandpa knew how important it was to chart the course, and all day, with intense focus and clarity, he had vigilantly documented our location. Like a watchman manning a post, he was well aware that he was responsible for the safety of his son and grandsons. He was in charge, and he knew it.

So often as men we forget that God has placed us in the very same place. We are the captain of our ship. Like my grandfather assuming the role of responsibility for us, we men must do the same for our families or anyone who is depending on us. Whether it is a nineteen-foot fishing boat or the *Titanic,* we average Joes stand the watch.

This reminds me of the Marine foot soldier who nighthawks for his buddies. He is an average Joe. While others with higher rank make decisions that affect thousands, he watches over a few. Alone in the dark, he stands his ground, always vigilant, always faithful: *no one is going to hurt my friends, my family, during my watch.*

You and I are no different. We have been given the mantle of authority to lead and guide others. God has entrusted us with a tremendous and honorable responsibility. Heaven is our home; this temporary place we live called earth is not. Our job is to do whatever it takes to make sure our families or anyone else we are responsible for makes it home.

As Grandpa pointed our little fishing boat into the wind, I asked, "How do you know which way is home, Grandpa?"

"Don't worry, Grandson. I will have you in the bay before supper," he hollered over the howl of the motor and the roar of the wind. The cold spray of the whitecaps stung our face as we gained speed. We were on a reciprocal southwestern course of 140 degrees. Grandpa knew that as long as we held that heading exactly, as long as we didn't waver more than a degree or two, we would make it to Trinidad Head, the entrance to the bay. The fight to get home had begun.

Wind gusts of forty to fifty miles per hour drove angry seawater into our faces and collected in the bottom of the boat. Waves at times reaching fifteen feet lifted us to the top of huge rollers, then we slid down into cavernous furrows. With walls of icy gray water enclosing us, there were moments when I thought we would never climb out of a deep trough. As we would approach the next rise, Grandpa would throttle up Big John in order to escape the trough and climb the advancing wave. At the top he would edge back on the power, knowing that the ride down the face of the gray behemoth would be the biggest challenge. Several times I cringed as white water built behind us, threatening to swamp the back of the boat. It's at times like these that Creation humbles a cocky fourteen-year-old. For a big Alaskan crab boat or a whaler, this would have been nothing. In our little boat, though, we were in a battle for our life.

With Dad and Grandpa at the helm, Toby and I sat clutching the backseats of the boat. Dad called out bearing corrections to Grandpa as they worked the boat forward. With each crashing wave and gust of wind, an adjustment had to be made to stay on course. Waves the size of hills pushed us in every direction. But after every wave, every effort of the storm to push us farther out to sea, Dad called out a course rectification, and Grandpa faithfully executed the change.

We were aiming for a mark miles to the southeast that represented safety, shelter, and warmth—an unseen bull's-eye that meant we would be home.

Fishermen and mariners in storms have long felt great comfort at the sound of a foghorn, that telltale signal from a floating buoy or a lighthouse on a point, announcing that the safety of the bay is close at hand. We were beaten, tired, and soaked when we all heard the faithful moan of the Trinidad Head foghorn. Still operational in 1974, this historic lighthouse was perched almost two hundred feet above the crashing sea. There are well-documented stories of how waves assaulted this structure in a historic 1913 storm, a testimony to the fury of the Pacific.

At almost the same moment that we heard the horn, we saw the soft glow of the 375-millimeter optic light cutting through the dense fog, just off our port side bow. We were home!

What a powerful sensation of safety, peace, and security I felt as we motored around towering Trinidad Head. Having reached the protection of the bay, we each let out a private sigh of relief. The water transformed from the tumult of the open ocean to the gentle ripple of the harbor.

A fisherman on the dock called out, "Hey, Ray! I see you've got your boys with you. How was the fishing?"

Grandpa never showed his hand when it came to fishing: "Oh, we brought in a few," he always said with a grin. Our fish hold could be stuffed to the top or as empty as the pantry before payday—it didn't matter. None of those guys ever really wanted to know how many fish we'd caught. It was all about the camaraderie shared among old salts of the sea.

We had caught a few this time, but more important, we had made it home safely with stories to tell and memories to lock away for a lifetime.

HITTING THE MARK

That night we sat around the fire, stuffed with fresh salmon, and reveled in the moment. Times like this make life rich and memorable. Hilary Cooper wrote, "Life is not measured by the number of breaths we take, but by the moments that take our breath away." I can still see my grandpa with a snort in his hand and his face lit by the fire, saying, "Boys, that was a day to remember!"

We never would have made it home if Grandpa hadn't stayed the course. Like an archer aiming for the target, we had to hit the mark. Grandpa knew that any deviation from the correct bearing would have meant certain disaster.

As men, we so often compromise. We rationalize in our mind that "it's only a little sin." No one will ever know. That voice whispers in our ear:

- "Come on, buddy. Everyone does it. So what if you cheat a little on your tax return?"
- "It really is no big deal that you take your secretary to an early dinner...to that really intimate little bistro on the coast. So what if you have a few drinks, tell an off-color joke or two, and marvel at the sunset. I mean, come on, dude, she really gets you. Your wife doesn't."
- "Who cares if you surf the Web and hang out for a bit on those sites that you know you shouldn't? You deserve a little break!"

Or do you?

Here's what the Bible has to say about this: "But now you must be holy in everything you do, just as God—who chose you to be his children—is holy.... And remember that the heavenly Father to whom you pray has no favorites when he judges. He will judge or reward you according to what you do. So you must live in reverent fear of him during your time as foreigners here on earth" (1 Peter 1:15, 17).

If my granddad had chosen to bend his resolve, to waver just a degree or two off course, we might not have made it home. For sure we would have ended up someplace not intended.

Life is that way. You and I are the men God has placed as a covering over our family and others. You and I, while we may just be average Joes, are the captains of our little boats. We are the ones who choose daily the direction we should take. We *choose* whether or not we are going to compromise the perfect direction God laid out for us in His Word. We may have the audacity to think that our compromise is no big deal or that no one will ever know. But the little concession today *will* have consequences tomorrow.

I let go of that memory from long ago as Mount Shasta came into view. Sadly, the cold dawn of reality drowned out the warm memories of a day spent fishing long ago.

As I continued my drive to my aunt's home, I wondered how my grandpa, my friend, would be. Would he remember me? Had the cancer stolen his mind as well as his body?

After I pulled into the drive and was hugged by Aunt Dolores and Uncle Jim, we made our way to Grandpa's room. "He has been asking when you would be coming," my aunt said. When I was a boy, Aunt Dolores had been my favorite. She always was full of joy, warmth, and an infectious zest for life. She and Uncle Jim are a strong example of a marriage lived at the foot of the Cross, what a godly marriage should look like.

Rounding the corner to Grandpa's bedroom, I was greeted with his strong smile and deep voice: "There's my grandson!" Tears filled my eyes as, moving to his side, I was given the hug that only a grandfather can give. For a long moment, time stood still as I held my dear, frail friend, the patriarch of our family, my pa, close. "It's so good to see you, boy," his ancient voice declared. "It's good to see you too," I stuttered through emotion-strained vocal chords.

In the moments that followed, memories were shared, laughter filled the room, and I found out that my hard-living granddad had "come to terms with the Man upstairs." For all of his ninety-plus years, Grandpa had chosen to live outside the strong embrace of his Creator. His self-declaration that he was not a man worthy of the Cross had shattered only a few days earlier as Aunt Dolores sat at his side while he talked to Jesus.

I was amazed to hear her recount Grandpa's simple prayer. Like a child he had said, "Jesus, this is Ray. Now I know I haven't been the kind of man you would have wanted me to be, but if You will have me, I'd like it if You would come into old Ray's heart." I can only imagine the uproar in heaven when that old Irishman asked God to clear out the dust and cobwebs of his broken, tired heart and fill it anew as only our Savior can. Aunt Dolores later told me that when Grandpa was done, he opened his eyes and, through great tears, asked her, "Did I do okay?" She answered through her own tears, "Yeah, Dad, you did great."

Grandpa had come home.

Stay the Course

In the days that followed, I spent as many hours as I could at Grandpa's side. We shared stories, laughed, and cried. Sometimes I just held his hand as he slept. In the early hours of evening, I would read Scripture to him as he drifted from this world to the next and back again. Although the pain of his cancer was severe, he seemed at peace.

I will never forget the time when I was a boy that Grandpa took on the stormy North Pacific and brought us home. He chose to stay on course, to not miss the mark, to do whatever it took to make sure his boys were safe.

The last day we shared together, I was given the opportunity to return the favor.

Grandpa's eternal destiny was already sealed. By his admission of sin and acceptance of the saving grace of Jesus Christ, he knew he was going to spend eternity in the incomprehensible creation of heaven. Yet in spite of Scripture's assurance of his salvation, Grandpa wanted to make sure the deal was sealed.

"Will you baptize your grandfather?" was the simple request from my aunt. "He has asked if you would." I couldn't believe my ears. Me? Are you kidding me? What an *unspeakable honor.* In the waning light of an early spring evening, as the sun began to drop below the horizon, I gently anointed my grandpa with water and prayed as he quietly spoke to his Creator.

My grandfather made sure a young boy made it home that stormy day on the North Pacific. He didn't miss the mark. He stayed the course. Years later that boy, now a man, another average Joe, did his best to see his granddad, his pa...home.

The course is before us. The storms of life are here. We are threatened every day by the winds of change, the tide of public opinion, and the breaking waves of moral decay. Yet, like my grandfather, we stand the watch. We, as men, must not compromise. While the storm rages, we bundle up our family, take the helm of our boat, and point the bow toward home.

6

The Soldier

The only thing necessary for evil to triumph is
for good men to do nothing.

— SIR EDMUND BURKE

WE SEE THEM EVERYWHERE. Whether it is at the airport, coffee
shop, or local barbershop, they cross our path almost every day. With
hair cut high and tight, the uniform, and an air of confidence born
from discipline and honor, they are the servicemen and women of
the United States Armed Forces. We admire them one and all.

From the crisp blues of the Marine honor guard to the whites of
the naval officer, each and every one of those serving in the military
is an expression of the uncompromising backbone of a great nation.

The men and women of the Army, Air Force, Coast Guard,
Navy, and Marines each stand the watch. They nighthawk 24/7 so
you and I can raise our kids in a country protected beneath the banner we call freedom. We are a safer country because Navy Seals,

Army Rangers, Marine Recon, Delta Force, Green Berets, Air Force Pararescue, and Coast Guard Rescue Swimmers each and every day take on missions that we often never hear about. From the blistering heat of the Middle East sands to rescue efforts in Haiti, Sri Lanka, and Mogadishu, from the rugged mountains of Afghanistan to the downtown streets of New Orleans after Hurricane Katrina, our brave servicemen and women fight honorably for freedom and the basic rights of humanity. They are the very best of us.

It was August 19, 1990. The massive C-5 Galaxy transport, filled with special operations Marines, vehicles, and equipment slowly climbed skyward through billowy white clouds and microbursts of rain. The four powerful General Electric turbofan engines strained to propel the giant, fully loaded four-hundred-ton plane skyward. Gaining altitude, the gray behemoth turned east for the continental United States.

Far below a beautiful young woman stood alone, scanning the sky for one last glimpse of the plane that carried Finn, her soon-to-be husband and my friend, off to the hot sands of the Middle East. Because of the nature of his deployment, the woman was unsure where her fiancé was going and when he would return. Like the hundreds of thousands of friends and family members who wave good-bye every year to departing soldiers, the ache of the unknown was setting in: *Would Finn come back? Would he survive his deployment? Would he be different when he returned? Would the horrors of combat forever change the man she'd just said good-bye to?*

Finn was a classic jarhead Marine. Troubled by a rough childhood, a lack of discipline in school, and a failed attempt at postgraduate athletics, this young average Joe—having nowhere else to go—sought a better life in the company of some of the country's best: the Marines. He did so well that he graduated first in his basic training class. With the title of "honor graduate," Finn earned the privilege of wearing dress blues at graduation.

The young Marine excelled at everything he set his mind to. In a short time the nowhere-to-go kid matured into a poster child for the corps. After months of hard work, Finn had earned the golden wings of a Recon Marine and joined the ranks of those highly trained patriots serving as Navy Seals, Army Rangers, and the Air Force Pararescue.

Finn was assigned to the First Marine Division for permanent duty. After months of intense training, he and his fellow teammates were about to put all their exhaustive preparations to the test. They were going to war.

The savage Iraqi dictator, Saddam Hussein, had brutally and without provocation ordered the invasion of Kuwait on August 2, 1990. His goal was the seizure of the rich oil fields of his peaceful southern neighbor. The United States responded with decisive force. Landing in northern Saudi Arabia on August 21, my friend—now a corporal—and his team were greeted with 133-degree heat on the tarmac as the nose cone of the C-5 opened to allow the squad and its equipment to evacuate the plane. Finn carried his life on his back knowing that he might never return home again. Everything he would need "in country" was neatly and methodically stowed away in the rucksack slung over his shoulder. Wearing his Kevlar helmet and carrying tactical gear and weapons, Finn made his way confidently down the steel ramp.

For the next three days, life for the team revolved around an exchange of information and the classic "bullets, beans, and Band-Aids" preparations for the upcoming insertion into the desert. That first night in Saudi, Finn and the other Marines tried to sleep under a poncho tied to the side of a Humvee, but the anticipation of the mission kept them all tossing and turning.

Long-buried emotions came to the surface for the young soldier. He recalled how prior to becoming a Recon Marine, he'd sat in the office of a Marine Corps colonel who'd quickly had enough of this young punk's attitude. "Son," he said with a booming voice, "you are either going to pass these tests or you're going to be a cook or pot scrubber your entire six-year tour here at the corps. Your choice." Nothing more was said. Finn had a choice to make, and he chose to be a Recon Marine. That grizzled old colonel would never know the life change he afforded my friend in that very moment.

MEN ON A MISSION

On the hot asphalt, Finn and hundreds like him were gearing up. They were ready at a moment's notice to put their lives on the line for a country and a people they might never know, yet only a few short days before these young soldiers had been playing Frisbee on the beach, enjoying a backyard barbecue, training on the base, or raising a young family. And now they were in a war zone. What is it that burns within a young man that would cause him to leave his home and family and possibly give his life for something he believes in?

Looking at pictures Finn had kept over the years, I saw the faces of young men like the guy next door who services your car or mows your lawn. With names like Mike, Joe, or Bill, these young men are average Joes who with honor have sought to do the right thing—to be the guy who will stand the watch for the defenseless and broken. These are the ones who choose to walk the streets of a battle-broken neighborhood in a far-off country just to make sure the people there are safe.

That's what average Joes do. Without fanfare, they roll up

their sleeves and get to the task at hand, no matter what it is. Finn and his team were getting ready to fight a war. You may just be dealing with a broken washing machine, a crabby boss, or a prideful teenager. It doesn't matter. Each of us has a job to do, no matter what it may be.

Two days later the orders came. The team was inserted a few kilometers from the Saudi-Kuwaiti border.

For the next five months, these and other special operations soldiers completed classified missions all over the Middle East in preparation for and during the execution of the massive U.S. air war. Finn and his unit worked feverishly at intelligence gathering for the allied forces command. Dug in deep and only a stone's throw from enemy lines, Finn's unit was critical to the success of the air campaign and foundational in the planning of the inevitable ground attack.

Saddam's forces had taken staggering losses and were now mounting an enormous assault on allied forces in a final, last-ditch attempt to keep control of Kuwait by invading Saudi Arabia. In the early morning hours of January 29, 1991, Iraq's First and Fifth Mechanized and Third Armored Divisions began moving south along the coastline of Kuwait into Saudi Arabia near the town of Kafji, which was directly in front of Finn's position.

On this suprisingly cold January morning, the intensity of the mission changed. The American-led air campaign had been devastating, but the realization that the impending ground war was about to begin heightened the awareness of Finn's entire team. In that moment the young men, some mere teenagers, recognized for sure that they were soldiers, average Joes fighting together for the lives of one another and for a people they would probably never meet. No longer did it matter who was a Marine jarhead, an Army dog, or a Navy booter. They all had a job to do. Without fanfare, they were about to get to it.

Honor...Integrity...Character

Often we overlook ordinary men and women in the Bible who accomplished extraordinary deeds. In the face of certain defeat, trials,
or even death, time and again these average Joes rose to the occasion
to surprise us with their wisdom, loyalty, and courage. It is easy to
remember men like King David, the apostle Paul, and John the Bap-
tist. But how easily we forget others, particularly men who existed in
the shadows, yet by their example of how they lived, they gave us an
example to follow—even today.

Uriah, a simple foot soldier in King David's army, is one of these.
A man living in the shadow of the great ones, Uriah exemplified
courage and loyalty in the face of certain death.

The book of 2 Samuel tells the story of a king's fall from glory.
In the spring, "when kings go to war" (11:1), David's army was at
war with the Ammonites. Joab, the army commander, was about to
lead the battle. A brilliant strategist and a fearless fighter, Joab never
lost a campaign. While an incredible leader and loyal friend, his
downfall was his ruthless, unquestioning devotion to David. Here
are the story's details:

> Late one afternoon David got out of bed after taking a nap
> and went for a stroll on the roof of the palace. As he looked
> out over the city, he noticed a woman of unusual beauty
> taking a bath. He sent someone to find out who she was,
> and he was told, "She is Bathsheba, the daughter of Eliam
> and the wife of Uriah the Hittite." Then David sent for
> her; and when she came to the palace, he slept with her....
> Then she returned home. Later, when Bathsheba discovered
> that she was pregnant, she sent a message to inform David.
> (11:2–5)

Pretty simple picture here: rich guy with everything steals the wife of an average Joe. He sleeps with her, defiling everything sacred in her marriage, then she becomes pregnant with his child. David's hormones had gotten him into quite a pickle, and now he needed to cover his tracks—his sin.

So David sent word to Joab: "Send me Uriah the Hittite." When Uriah arrived, David asked him how Joab and the army were getting along and how the war was progressing. Then he told Uriah, "Go on home and relax." David even sent a gift to Uriah after he had left the palace. But Uriah wouldn't go home. He stayed that night at the palace entrance with some of the king's other servants.

When David heard what Uriah had done, he summoned him and asked, "What's the matter with you? Why didn't you go home last night after being away for so long?"

Uriah replied, "The Ark and the armies of Israel and Judah are living in tents, and Joab and his officers are camping in the open fields. How could I go home to wine and dine and sleep with my wife? I swear that I will never be guilty of acting like that."

"Well, stay here tonight," David told him, "and tomorrow you may return to the army." So Uriah stayed in Jerusalem that day and the next. Then David invited him to dinner and got him drunk. But even then he couldn't get Uriah to go home to his wife. Again he slept at the palace entrance. (11:6–13)

Honor…integrity…character. Such were the qualities of the soldier Uriah. Given the choice to go home and be with his wife, the warrior chose to stay with the king's servants. Given the option of rest and pleasure, a choice that would be absolutely understandable, Uriah chose honor instead. In an attempt to cover his sin, David worked hard to get this simple man to compromise what was right. Uriah the soldier would not budge. Simple dedication to principle, to doing what was right, was one quality of Uriah the man.

There are times in life when adhering to our principles can make existence difficult. We sometimes find ourselves at the wrong end of a joke. Or maybe we lose a business deal or a so-called friend. In an extreme situation, sticking to a principle might cost us our lives. Such was the case for Uriah:

> So the next morning David wrote a letter to Joab and gave it to Uriah to deliver. The letter instructed Joab, "Station Uriah on the front lines where the battle is fiercest. Then pull back so that he will be killed." So Joab assigned Uriah to a spot close to the city wall where he knew the enemy's strongest men were fighting. And Uriah was killed along with several other Israelite soldiers. (11:14–17)

Add murder to David's list of wrongdoings.

Uriah the soldier, full of honor and principle, did what he was told. He obeyed his superior in the face of certain death. Uriah could have run away but instead chose honor. He chose to fight. In the big scheme of things, he was a blip on the screen, a nobody, a scapegoat for a king. Yet in the bigger picture, Uriah the Hittite was an average Joe who chose dignity and integrity.

The Ultimate Sacrifice

Centuries later, a small group of Marine foot soldiers—"grunts"— would courageously choose to sacrifice everything for honor and the brotherhood of soldiers. They would give their lives to make sure others made it home safely.

In the early morning hours of January 29, 1991, just three kilometers from the border of Kuwait, Finn's recon team was dug in right in front of what was potentially Iraq's main point of attack. At approximately 0200 hours, Finn's small Marine platoon, now on high alert, received a radio warning that an estimated one hundred armored Iraqi battle vehicles were bearing down on them. Flying high above, a remotely powered vehicle (RPV) had spotted the advancing Iraqi assault force.

Instructed by command to prepare to leave but for now to hold fast, the small special ops contingent quickly dismantled their outpost. At that moment, discipline, honor, and the code so deeply burned into the heart of a Marine took over. Men of any age would be hard pressed to stay put in a sand hole while thousands of tons of enemy hardware bore down on them, but these Marines followed orders and didn't budge.

We sometimes forget, while living our predictable and comfortable lives, that deep within each of us burns the passion and desire to do something that will set us apart to face and survive an impossible circumstance. These were mere kids, dug in deep, with chins set squarely in defiance of the oncoming assault.

Their situation appeared hopeless: Thousands of miles from home, a handful of young Americans stared unflinchingly into the savage gun barrels of oncoming armored Iraqi aggressors. Saddam's main battle tank, the Russian-made T-72, could shoot sixty-pound shells up to a staggering nine thousand yards. In the darkness, the rumble of the turbocharged diesel engines of those tanks could be heard a mere three kilometers away.

Suddenly the sky exploded. Without warning, red and green flares erupted from three sides of the dug-in squad. A small patrol of the First Marine Division had rushed forward and engaged the enemy. In order to distinguish friendly from enemy fire, the Marines had released red and green flares to determine battle lines. In front and on both sides, soldiers were fighting to protect the recon team. That small contingent of Special Operation Marines could see their fellow jarheads taking on the enemy. On all sides the battle raged. With the enemy engaged in three directions, the only route of escape was to the south. The order from command came over the radio: "Evacuate the team and all equipment immediately." With their fellow Marines still engaging the enemy, the team reluctantly loaded their Hummers.

As I interviewed Finn, the pain of that searing moment was still deeply etched in his face. While a Marine never questions orders, the memory of leaving the battle and of what came next has always haunted him.

Finn is a tough guy. No matter how you size him up, he is a man of steadfast resolve, grit, and passion. At five foot ten, he is as wide as he is tall. He is not a fellow I would ever want to cross paths with. Yet emotions run deep in the heart of an average Joe. The only time I have ever seen my friend lose it emotionally was while he recounted the rest of this story.

With all their equipment loaded, the fifty-caliber machine guns on top of the Hummers manned, and everyone cocked and locked, the team began the brutally slow extraction. With lights out, they navigated by moonlight and the small illuminated slits cut in the metal that covered the Humvees' headlights. Still fighting to protect the withdrawal of Finn's team, the contingent of Marines behind them continued their valiant assault on the approaching enemy. But like a collapsing horseshoe, Iraq's menacing force slowly closed the only route of escape.

With tears in his weathered eyes, my friend shared with me the radio chatter between a Marine officer in one light armored vehicle and his troops in another. "They were incredibly professional, Troy, as they talked back and forth during the battle," Finn recounted. "They knew what they were doing, they knew where they were, they had the battle in hand. Then, without warning, one of the two radios went silent." In that moment my friend, too, went silent. "I can still hear that officer, a young captain, calling out over and over to his troops. They weren't there anymore. In a split second they were gone."

Finn bowed his head low to the table as he spoke. "In that instant, Marines...fellow soldiers...men I will never know...died to get me home."

Soldiers do that. Average Joes do that.

Finn vividly recalled the moment he walked off the commercial airliner that flew him home many months later. As he stood on the tarmac in the embrace of his young fiancée, the memory of that night still burned in his heart—the heart of a Recon Marine. Through a few well-earned tears, he breathed a quiet thank-you to his Maker as he held his future in his arms. He was home.

The men who sacrificed everything that cold night were not noteworthy. They were foot soldiers, jarheads, or—some would say—mere grunts. They were probably young, in battle for the first time, full of promise. Yet when the time came to lay it on the line, they did so with honor and dignity. Fighting far from home, those brave young Marines kept their end of the deal. With chiseled chins, these average Joes defiantly held their ground. They were—and forever will be—the very best of us all.

After my interview with my friend Finn on that cold, rainy day, I walked back to my truck keenly aware of my surroundings, of the place I call home. The sidewalks of our little town were full of afternoon shoppers, businessmen, and young people. I wondered, Do they know? Do they fully appreciate the freedoms we take for granted? Does the kid with his pants pulled halfway down his butt understand that *young men his age died in battle? Does he even care? Does the young couple driving the car with the "Peace Not War" bumper sticker understand that freedom is not free?*

The freedoms we so easily take for granted were afforded our country by the sacrificial blood of men and women who have gone on before us.

This old cowboy tips his hat to honor them, the very best of us all—the soldiers, airmen, and sailors of the United States Armed Forces.

7

The Cowboy

Courage is being scared to death
but saddling up anyway.

—JOHN WAYNE

I THINK THAT MOST EVERY GUY, at some point in his life, has
dreamed of being a cowboy.

If, like me, you grew up in the years of the spaghetti westerns,
Roy Rogers, Lorne Greene, and *The Rifleman,* your Christmas
stocking overflowed with toy six-guns, Gene Autry books, and the
venerable Daisy Red Ryder BB gun. Our childhood dreams reso-
nated with the images we watched on the silver screen. We thought
that a six-gun and a horse called Red solved every problem and
earned us the respect of those around us.

We dreamed of riding the range from Canada to Mexico...of
watching the sunset over golden fields of grass...of herding cattle
across the great plains of Kansas, through the canyons of Moab and
the high mountain valleys of the Rockies.

In the late 1950s and through the '60s and '70s, Saturday mati-nees in theaters around the country filled to capacity as moviegoers watched the consummate cowboy chase down the bad guys and save the rancher's beautiful daughter. With popcorn, Milk Duds, and soda in hand, we marveled at the tall, larger-than-life man on the big screen:

John Wayne, a.k.a. the Duke.

Just the mention of that iconic name conjures up images of a big man on an even bigger horse. With a Colt .45 at his side, his trusty Winchester 1873 in the saddle scabbard, and a hat bigger than Texas, John Wayne rode from the flickering silver screen of the local movie house into the hearts of little boys all across America. He sat tall in the saddle, no matter what happened to him. And no matter how bad the situation was, that old boy would never back down, never compromise, never give up.

If you were a bad guy, your days were numbered. His yes was yes, his no was no. If he didn't like you, he told you so. With a hand-shake from the Duke, the agreement was made, the promise was sure. There was no need for some silly piece of paper with his signa-ture on it.

He was a brawler, a horseman, and a legend. *John Wayne had sand.*

While I realize, of course, that the characters John Wayne por-trayed on the big screen were the creations of scriptwriters, John Wayne, the man, was not unlike those he portrayed. History records that, in his heart of hearts and in spite of his imperfect humanity, the Duke was a cowboy.

You may be asking yourself, *So what is Troy up to now? Why in the world would he write a chapter about cowboys? Isn't the whole cow-boy thing kind of "yesterday"?*

Well, here's why I'm giving space to the breed: I believe the life values lived out by true cowboys—men of grit, determination, principle, faith, and trust—are the very qualities every man, every average Joe, should wrap himself around each day of his life. Anchored deep within the heart of the cowboy are values that help a man weather the ferocious storms of everyday life.

Sadly, today those ideals are becoming rare. The newspapers I read, the nightly news broadcasts, the television shows I watch, and even what I see within the walls of my local church show that steadfast values and morals have withered under the destructive assault of concession. We are bombarded every day with stories of men who chose the easy road, the wide highway of compromise, self-centeredness, and arrogance. Many travel this superhighway. Fewer men choose the narrow, winding yet high road of truth, authenticity, and resolve.

Jesus said, "You can enter God's Kingdom only through the narrow gate. The highway to hell is broad, and its gate is wide for the many who choose the easy way. But the gateway to life is small, and the road is narrow, and only a few ever find it'" (Matthew 7:13–14).

Too few men determine within themselves to live a life marked by purpose, wisdom, gentle strength, and unwavering faithfulness. These are the guys traveling on the high road. It saddens me, too, that I often have turned onto the highway of societal correctness, selfish sin, pride, and compromise when I should have driven hard on the two-lane road of certainty, of moral determination.

A REAL COWBOY

For most of us, the dream of being a cowboy was just that—a dream. For a chosen few, the life they live is that of…the cowboy.

Clint was, and is, one of the lucky ones a cowboy. Born to a simple family deep in the high desert country of eastern Oregon, Clint is slight of build, has hands of iron, and makes you smile with his sharp but friendly wit. He wears his boots well.

As far back as he can remember, horses and cattle have been a part of his daily life. While most boys at his age ran through the house straddling a stick horse, Clint grew up with a rope in one hand and reins in another while tending cattle on his father's small ranch. At four years old, he was introduced to what became a lifetime partnership: the cowboy and his horse. His first ride was a small red dun pony named Sarah. Clint's boyhood learning environment taught him hard work and the values of honesty, loyalty, and temperance.

While Clint is and always will be a cowboy, it is the heart condition of the man, this average Joe, that causes me to write of him and his kind.

In conversations with Clint, I've found his explanations of the cowboy way always simple and brief: "The world around us has gotten so cluttered, so busy, so…noisy," Clint mused one day over a cup of coffee. We were getting ready for a ride out west of our ranch and had stopped to get a bite to eat at a small diner in Tumalo. Clint went on, "We have forgotten what really matters in life. We fill up space with words when none are needed. Men work so hard to get their point across, their views, even trying to bring validation to their lives. No one listens anymore because everyone talks too much."

I nodded. Neither of us spoke for a couple of minutes, content to savor the eggs, bacon, and coffee.

"Even more troubling is the lack of substance in what is said," Clint continued. "Why would I want to listen to conversations centered on…nothing? My grandpa was a man of few words. But when he did talk, we as children listened because what he had to say meant something."

The Wise Listen

My friend Clint was so right. If you take the time to listen to the conversations going on around you, it is easy to see how so much of what is spoken, especially between men, is nothing more than prideful window dressing. It can go something like this:

"How you doin', Bob?" George casually asks his next-door neighbor.

"Good. Real good. Got a new Audi ordered. Loaded with all the good stuff!" Bob proudly puffs up his chest as he brags about his recent acquisition. "What about you?" Bob has set the stage for the two gladiators to grapple in today's arena of one-upmanship.

George, with his chest equally puffed up, responds, "New Audi, huh? That's great, Bob. Yep, things are great. Got the corner office all to myself this past week. I'm sure the firm will be begging me to become a partner before the end of the year."

Bob counters, "Partner? That's super, George. You would make a good one. I've been a partner in our firm for over a year now. The benies are great."

And so the conversation goes. On and on the two modern-day combatants counter each other, never really asking about anything that would foster true friendship.

Listen, men, I am not trying to set the stage for some deep, introspective, "discover our feelings" thing here. Guys are guys. Sometimes we just need to grunt, share a cold one, and talk about nothing deeper than last week's football game or where the steelhead trout are running. I get that. However, if you asked your neighbor Tom how things were going and he responded with, "Sally has cancer," or "I am getting a divorce," or "I got fired last week and we don't know what we're going to do," would you have built the kind of relationship with him to be a true friend in that critical moment? Would you know what to say? Would you even care?

I ask myself the same questions. Have I spent so much time with my buddies just filling space with words that I don't have the kind of friendship that's strong enough to weather the storms when they come? If Bob or George or whoever actually cracked open his heart in a time of desperation, would I be able to respond in a manner worthy of a friend?

In the books of Proverbs and Ecclesiastes, books rich in simple cowboy wisdom, Solomon speaks over and over of the futility of too many words, calling the man who talks too much a fool. The wise old king reminds us that fools talk a lot; the wise listen.

"Generally you ain't learnin' nothing when your mouth's a-jawin'," an unknown author said.

The Important Things in Life

With our late-morning breakfast finished, Clint and I gathered our gear and, with our horses in the trailer, pointed my old Dodge truck west toward the foothills of the Three Sisters Wilderness.

Nestled just below the icy, snow-covered peaks of the Three Sisters Mountains sits an area we fondly call "the reservoir." At the east end of over eight hundred square miles of wild Oregon, the reservoir is a starting point for countless riding experiences I have enjoyed over the years. Kim and I have hiked, trained for marathons, explored, and ridden horses all over the ponderosa pine–covered foothills of this treasured area.

With the sun at our left shoulders, Clint and I headed west, with Clint on my horse Eclipse, and me on a big palomino gelding named Jed. At a touch over sixteen hands and thirteen hundred pounds, Jed is the picture of a big man's horse. Saddled with my Billy Cook buckaroo saddle, the rawboned gelding looks like a horse a graying cowboy like me would ride.

Few words were spoken as we made our way up into the hills. For several hours we zigzagged through stands of pine and fir trees. Sometimes on trails, most of the time not, we let the horses pick their way higher and higher into wilderness.

At times like these I am hard-pressed to imagine how life could be any better.

Sometimes we talked; sometimes we just rode. The majesty of the creation all around silenced us. It was early spring, and signs of new life were beginning to peek out from winter's icy embrace. Tufts of fescue grass were turning green. Delicate high-mountain wild-flowers were breaking through soft, soggy earth. Even though the sun was shining, I was glad in the spring chill to have my Carhartt coat and batwing chaps. The remnant of winter's final hurrah was felt in the wind. When the late afternoon sun began to creep behind the crystal peak of the North Sister, we turned back for home.

"Just what are the important things in your life?" I asked Clint. "What would you say are the things that drive you to be who you are?"

He didn't hesitate. "We get so worked up over the things that never matter, when the important things in life are right in front of us," Clint said. "My faith, my family, and good friends. The rest is just salt on the steak."

His point was well taken. There is nothing else that really matters in life.

I have heard the stories, as have you, of dying men wishing they had spent less time at the office and more with their family. We agree with those who counsel us to cultivate good, deep, abiding friendships with those around us. We nod our heads and beat our chests in agreement, yet few of us ever take on the life-changing challenge of making the first things...*first.*

I chimed in, repeating to Clint the greatest commandment of all: "'You must love the Lord your God with all your heart, all your soul, all your strength, and all your mind.' And, 'Love your neighbor as yourself'"(Luke 10:27). We both chuckled, knowing that in those profound words there was no mention of career, a bigger house or faster car, the corner office, or the size of a bank account. God's Word, like the heart of a cowboy, is quite simple. Jesus summed it up: *Love the Lord and your friend.*

The rest? Well, the rest is noise.

Cowboys get it. Yes, I know, they are men just like you and me, each with his own faults and troubles. Here I am almost deifying the breed when they, like the rest of us, can be beer-drinking, cussing, womanizing boneheads too. In fact, Clint spoke of quitting the rodeo circuit as a bareback bronco rider for that very reason. Suffice it to say, while all that's true, the cowboy in his heart of hearts, at the very center of his soul, is a solid, trustworthy, hard-working man of simple values and intrepid faith.

Rounding the last bend toward the horse trailer, my very being was filled to the brim. What a day! Time spent in the grasp of the mountains carves deep memories into my soul. And to share it with a man, a cowboy, like Clint—that was icing on the cake.

With the horses loaded in the trailer, we made our way back to the ranch. Not much was said. Words were unnecessary. The day spoke for itself.

Clint will never live in a big house, drive a fancy car, or retire with a fat 401(k). He, like me, will probably work right up until the time he meets his Maker. Yet in the arena of what really matters, Clint is rich beyond imagination. With the love of an extraordinary wife, a small home resonating with the laughter of five children, and the love of God, my friend lives each day in the arena of truth, honesty, and integrity. Within his simple yet rock-solid heart beats compassion for his family, a valiant devotion to his country, and an unwavering zeal for Jesus Christ.

So should it be with us all.

8

The Mentor

THE UNCOMPROMISING, STEADFAST apostle Paul is near the end of his life. Years of ministry to the early church have taken their toll on this man chosen by God to minister to the Gentiles. He is finishing the race set before him. His work nears completion.

In his final letter to the growing church, he directs his attention to his friend, companion, "son," and student, Timothy. Here's how his last-known letter to Timothy begins:

> This letter is from Paul, an apostle of Christ Jesus by God's will, sent out to tell others about the life he has promised through faith in Christ Jesus.
>
> It is written to Timothy, my dear son.
>
> May God our Father and Christ Jesus our Lord give you grace, mercy, and peace.
>
> Timothy, I thank God for you. (2 Timothy 1:1–3)

Over and over in this short epistle, Paul shows his deep compassion and love for the young man of faith. Recruited by Paul not long after the apostle's disappointing separation from John Mark, Timothy has worked tirelessly for years at Paul's side. They were together when new believers discovered the saving grace of Jesus Christ as well as when the gospel was distorted and rejected. Through tears of laughter and sorrow, through suffering and great victory, these redoubtable men of the faith have worked side by side in their audacious development of the early church.

And Paul loved the young man as if he were his own son:

> I have no one else like Timothy, who genuinely cares about your welfare. All the others care only for themselves and not for what matters to Jesus Christ. But you know how Timothy has proved himself. Like a son with his father, he has helped me in preaching the Good News. (Philippians 2:20–22)

They experienced it all—together. Paul the mentor, Timothy the student.

While the apostle Paul had many extraordinary accomplishments, his calling as a mentor to Timothy became foundational in the furthering of the gospel long after Paul was gone. The tactical, pragmatic, and passionate wisdom of the older man was handed down to the younger ambassador of the faith. Not unlike a runner who had passed the baton, Paul, through Timothy, was able to continue his work after his death.

Mentors—men of wisdom and passion who are usually older—are all around us. We find them working part time at Home Depot or looking at some tackle at the local fly shop. They are elders in our churches, Boy Scout leaders, and volunteers at local charities. Most of them don't understand Blu-ray players, iPods, or Facebook. I guess they would rather talk with you face to face than through some "confounded computer." Today's music, movies, and television shows cause them to shudder as they realize how different life is today. They often scratch their heads in trying to understand "kids these days." When young, their nights out on the town were filled with dancing to "Moonlight Serenade," "In the Mood," "Hound Dog," and "Blueberry Hill." They knew the waltz, the jitterbug, the lindy, and the swing. They drank chocolate malts, drove cars with rumble seats, and fought in Vietnam, Korea, and the Big One.

Most are the wise, gray-haired, elderly men whom we so often overlook as we go blindly through life. Sadly, sometimes men of advanced years are forced into the shadows of existence, the background of all that goes on around us. If we leave them in the back alleys of humanity, we risk the loss of the wisdom, integrity, and honor of these men whose being has been forged in the furnace of life's experiences.

They have worked hard, raised families, started businesses, and honored the marriage vows of their youth. Today, when staying married to one wife seems almost prudish and outdated, these men enjoy the fruit of a life spent with one woman. We are staggered when they proudly exclaim that for forty, fifty, even sixty years they have stood with the woman they love. Words like *covenant, honor, perseverance,* and *loyalty* are the hallmarks of these men. Our nation is stronger, more moral, and steadfast because of them.

Such is the legacy of my friend Kep. Born when times were simpler, quieter, and uninterrupted by the clamor of cell phones, satellite television, e-mails, and the Internet, Kep, now in his seventies, grew up in the nostalgic but rambunctious 1940s and '50s. Dr. Seuss, the Slinky, Lionel trains, and the prized Daisy Red Ryder BB gun were the toys that filled the hearts of young boys in those days. As a young man growing up with Frank Sinatra, Marilyn Monroe, Lucky Strike cigarettes, vinyl records, and the Korean War, Kep experienced a country still strong, still faithful, still moral.

Even while I was growing up in the tumultuous sixties, life was different than it is today. *Entitlement* was not in our vocabulary or worldview. If you wanted something, you worked for it. The American Dream was there for the taking, if you chose to roll up your sleeves and earn it. For my father, work was six days a week. Sunday was for church and his family. For Pete's sake, back then we even respected our teachers, said the Pledge of Allegiance, and prayed in school!

Kep is an average Joe. In my opinion, most qualified mentors are. While a highly intelligent and accomplished man, Kep keeps his passions simple and honorable. He embraces life with an intense devotion to family, love of the outdoors, and an unbridled commitment to Jesus Christ. For Kep, life is an adventure to be savored every day, which brings the promise of life at its richest and most beautiful. While not perfect, Kep exudes a zeal for each day in honor of the One who saved him. His passion for the King completely qualifies him to lead other men, to be a mentor. It is that ardor and his love of life that draws me to his side.

Kep is a warrior of the faith.

I want to be just like him.

EXPERIENCE LIFE TOGETHER

The mentoring of one man by another is an interesting journey. Before one considers becoming a mentor or submitting to one, many questions must be answered, for to be a mentor—the life tutor of another man—is a solemn responsibility. To submit to the leading of another man is a profound decision. While both roles of mentor and student are equally serious in nature, the life change afforded each is fascinating and fulfilling.

What was the key to Paul and Timothy's relationship that fostered such ageless success in them both? What does it mean to be a mentor? What qualities should we look for in a man we would trust to help guide us through the seemingly endless potholes of manhood? For a mentor, how old is old enough? What skills are required? What is required of the student?

I have often thought that mentoring was a formal, structured, almost scientific endeavor, that being a mentor required many scholastic achievements, business success, marital bliss, and the perspective of an ancient sage. And that, likewise, to be under the tutelage of another man would require me to be the perfect student.

Over the years I have learned that neither stereotype makes much practical sense. No man is either the perfect student or the textbook tutor. I have learned that the mentoring process *is* the journey. Through multiple mistakes over the years, I have learned that faith, honesty, integrity, commitment, and a genuine love for each other are the critical cornerstones to mentoring. The time-proven foundation of experiencing life together, either as the teacher or the student, is one that every man should be a part of. And, yes, even average Joes, men without all the supposed "right stuff," can be instrumental in the leadership of others. In fact, the very best mentors are those who would be considered average Joes.

A few years ago, my friend Kep unknowingly took on the responsibility of mentoring a tired, somewhat calloused, selfish, and prideful man: me. It was December 2008, and Kim and I had traveled south from Bend to northern California to spend some time with Kep and his wife, Katie. Over the years, each had become dear to Kim and me. Both of them, through the grace and love of Jesus Christ, filled longstanding and troubling vacancies in our hearts.

For several days we reveled in laughter, stories by the fire, bountiful food, spirited discussion over episodes of *24*, and simple silence in the couple's presence. However, rain had kept us inside, and Kep and I were dying to get to the lake and fish. I mean, come on, guys! Good food and fellowship are fantastic…but *fishing?* Well, it's hard to top a day on the lake. While the rain poured, hour after hour, we looked longingly at Kep's old fishing boat, slowly filling to the gunwale with rainwater, and hoped the deluge would lessen enough for us to get a line in the water.

On the fourth day, the downpour eased. With fishing poles stored, the outboard motor fueled, and some of Katie's homemade goodies in the ice chest, we left the house as the skies promised a banner day on Shasta Lake. Just ten miles north of Redding, Shasta Lake is a renowned gathering place for water-skiers, vacationers, and fishermen from all over the Northwest. Full of rainbow trout, brown trout, bass, and the occasional chinook salmon, the lake is an incredible spot to spend a day, especially in the company of a good friend.

Until this day, Kep and I had never enjoyed any extended time together, just the two of us. We'd been friends, but I had never really gotten to know this wise and gentle man, this average Joe. That was about to change.

It has always amazed me how the simple sport of fishing can deeply restore a man. Growing up with a fishing pole in my hand, I became keenly aware of the healing power of catching fish.

For several hours, while trolling across the lake under a broken sky of clouds and sun, Kep and I shared story after story about life. We laughed at how we men can be such pigheaded idiots, how often we are so driven in arenas of life that really don't matter much. Kep generously cracked open his aged heart to share his failures as a husband and as a man. I, too, responded with stories of regret. We allowed ourselves moments of painful introspection, only to mentally crawl out of the emotional pit to see the God-given good in us both.

I have become skeptical of the guy who seems to be forever condemning himself as a man. You know the type: he always arrives at your men's prayer breakfast or gathering with another tearful failure or regret. While it is good for us to get the garbage out, Jesus died on the cross to set us free from our past and our weaknesses. The apostle Paul wrote, "What this means is that those who become Christians become new persons.... The old life is gone. A new life has begun!" (2 Corinthians 5:17). The man you and I were before we received the cleansing blood of Jesus exists no longer.

Kep and I spoke of past regrets only to swell with joy, knowing that we were forgiven. We spoke of salvation, the joy of life in Christ, the blessing of a good wife. We embraced the notion that we were better men because of the wives God had given us. Then, over cards and coffee in the wheelhouse, I truly realized what it means to be a mentor. It's not rocket science! Mentoring is an older, mature man of faith sharing life in Jesus with a younger man of faith.

That day with Kep there were no formulas, no books to read, no structured conversation around a preplanned agenda. It was just truth, honesty, humility, and passion all wrapped up in a wonderful package for two weathered, somewhat crusty, plain, average guys to enjoy. We laughed, joked, and sometimes just watched the water as the boat trolled along. It was perfect. We caught fish. Well, Kep caught fish. I lost at the card games.

It was mentoring.

FIND A MENTOR...BE A MENTOR

There are many types of average Joe. Our backgrounds are as varied as can be imagined. We come wrapped in unique packages resulting from how we have lived. The ones who are weathered, wrinkled, and topped with gray hair are the desired mentors. Deep within each is an ancient sage full of wisdom waiting to be shared. Kep, with battered hands, wizened skin, and receding gray hair, poured years of wisdom into the heart of a younger man. From one average Joe to another, he afforded me the opportunity to sit at his side and learn the ways of maturity.

If you are reading this and fall into the category of mature, getting along in years, and a little worn around the edges, we younger men need you. Respectfully, I challenge you to find a "Timothy," to set aside time in your well-earned golden years to be a mentor to a junior brother. There are young men all around you who deeply desire the wisdom, grace, and temperance of an older, wiser man. I realize that the world has changed and that, in your mind, you may wonder what an "old geezer" like you has to offer some headstrong young man. Well, I can assure you that you have within you the very elixir that every young man desperately thirsts for. Brewed over years, in the belly of the cast-iron pot of your experience, is the compound of wisdom, temperance, courage, steadfastness, resolve, and humility. These and countless other traits that come with age are vital to the growing up of the next generation of men.

Think what would have happened to the early church if Paul and others like him had chosen not to pass the baton of leadership to the Timothys around them. Candidly, *nothing would have happened!* The church might have stopped dead in its tracks if mentors had chosen instead to retire and play golf and canasta and watch *SportsCenter* 24/7. These are not bad things, but such diversions should never replace the God-given responsibility for men to raise up the next generation.

And don't think you have to somehow be a perfect man of God! No, just be an honest, grateful, growing man of God—still in process.

On the other hand, if you are younger, full of promise, and lacking gray hair, then listen up: *find a mentor.*

Within your circle of existence waits a man who will be more valuable to you than gold. At church, in your neighborhood, or maybe even in your group of friends, he's there. His maturity could be your saving grace in keeping you from the pitfalls of selfishness, pride, arrogance, and self-destruction. Maybe you may think you have the world by the tail, but I'm here to tell you that the same tail can beat you senseless. Like a beacon of light in a storm, so is a mentor for you. Find him.

As I close this simple chapter, I offer what I consider critical standards for any mentoring relationship: *it's all or nothing.* For this to work, each man must commit to giving the other considerable time and effort. All good and healthy relationships take work.

- *Trust.* What is shared within the context of a mentoring relationship must be held in trust, with complete confidence.

- *Absolute honesty.* For there ever to be real health, real growth, and real depth, both must be committed to total openness and honesty.

- *Faith.* This is absolutely critical to true mentoring. Outside of a vibrant and growing relationship with Jesus Christ, mentoring in its purest sense can never happen. Yes, you can teach some young guy to build a 350 small-block Chevy, to fish, or to catch a football. While those are good and fun things, mentoring is different. Honest life change comes from our Creator. Like with Paul and Timothy, the real mentoring came in the context of their relationship with God.

Guys, life is so very short. To live as God intended is something I desperately want. I trust you do as well. Walking shoulder to shoulder with men of age and faith brings balance to imbalance, peace from chaos, and wisdom out of foolishness.

Masculine life shared in the company of a mentor is one of learning, discovery, and resolve. It is a life rich in the embrace and plan of our Creator.

(Written for Pastor Ken, Kep, and Grandpa Ray.)

THE CARPENTER
AND THE WOOD

9

The Friend

WITH A BRILLIANT SPLASH, the silver chrome–bodied, twelve-pound steelhead trout crashed earthward after its acrobatic antics high above the clear, icy green water.

It was an early morning in January. Southwestern Oregon had endured weeks of record-breaking Pacific Northwest winter weather. For hours the sky had threatened another storm as clouds forming over the ocean made their way inland. Heaven and earth were melting into one gray, cold, and wet winter day. With the temperature just above freezing, sleet began to fall. It was perfect weather for fishing winter steelhead!

My buddy Randy and I had journeyed to Bandon, Oregon, for a shot at hooking a big one. With Randy's brother, Jeff, on the oars of his drift boat, the three of us were floating our way down the icy waters of the south fork of the Coquille River. Known for its abundance of fish, the Coquille is world class when it comes to winter runs of massive steelhead trout.

With the mouth of the river running into the Pacific only a few miles downriver, the fish we were hunting had, more than likely, left the ocean only a few hours before. *Perfect.* They would reach the deep pools of our fishing grounds in pristine condition. On their way to spawn, far to the east, each mile of struggle up the river would deteriorate their condition. Like salmon, steelhead are anadromous: Born in freshwater rivers and streams, they travel to the ocean, where they mature. Later they leave the saltwater environment of the sea, spawn in the freshwater river or stream from which they came, and then return to the Pacific for another cycle. Steelhead undertake this journey many times; salmon, only once. The grueling journey, as well as the act of spawning, saps every ounce of energy and reserves of the fish.

Catching the winter run at the very peak of their condition is truly an incredible experience. On light tackle, steelhead of the Pacific Northwest can give an angler a once-in-a-lifetime thrill. The one at the end of my ten-pound-test line was doing just that. Every sense in me was on high alert as I worked to rein in the runaway freight train I had hooked. Each time I would crank back on the fighting fish, Randy would holler some testosterone-infused comment at me: "Lay the smack down on that big bad boy," or "Keep the line tight. Don't horse him; give him room to run. Okay…now… reel in!"

Like some crazed football coach rising from the cobwebs of my antiquated memory, Randy continued his armchair quarterbacking as I worked to get the big fish in. In one moment the fish would swim right at us as I frantically reeled in the line to keep the hook set. Then the ticked-off silver locomotive would about-face and make a full-on sprint for deeper water. This aggressive attempt at escape would strip dozens of yards off my screaming reel. Each time he would reach the relative safety of a deeper pool, I would crank the rod hard right or left, trying to keep him from going way down and getting leverage.

All three of us were yelling at one another, the fish, and whatever else we could holler at.

"I got him!"

"No, you don't!"

"You're gonna lose him in the deep!"

"No, I am not!"

"Come on, farm boy, get 'im to the shore!"

On and on it went, the priceless banter of friends.

That was a good day! It is an incredible thing to be in the company of good friends. But how rare it seems anymore.

WHY IS FRIENDSHIP SO HARD?

Companionship among men is an interesting thing. As boys, we were able to create and enjoy lasting friendships. We found it easy to shoulder up with other guys down the road. Our days were filled with building forts, hiking in the hills behind our homes, riding bikes, surfing, whatever. We explored what was available in our neighborhood. We had good times and bad. Sometimes we fought; sometimes we cried. We shared our deepest thoughts, biggest dreams, and supported one another when we failed. We shared a lot of things, but most of all, we just lived. We were friends.

I struggle sometimes with what has happened as we have grown up.

Long gone are those days of simplicity. Erased from our memories are the times when we just enjoyed the company of a friend. Why? Why is it so hard to experience life with other guys as we once did?

Now, don't get me wrong. I am not some forlorn fifty-year-old sap trying to relive his childhood. I am not the guy who still wears his letterman's jacket and high school ring and hangs out at the local burger joint trying to relive the sixties. I am aware, though, of how seemingly hard it is for most men to foster and live within the bonds of friendship with another man.

Why?

In a book about average Joes written by an average Joe, you are not going to get some psychobabble, Dr. Frankenstein answer. Candidly, I am not that smart. And I am for sure not going to tread down some tear-filled exploration into the recesses of a guy's mind and soul. I'm not going to pine over why we men find it hard to express ourselves; I'm not going to seek depth in a relationship because our mommies didn't hold us when we were babies or because our dads dropped us on our heads. Get over it! I am so incredibly sick and tired of the emasculation of men in our society. I see it every day—guys trying to get in touch with their feminine side. *We don't have a feminine side! We are guys!*

On the contrary, the simplistic comeback you are going to get here is probably worth no more than a cup of coffee at the local diner. It for certain is not worth the cost of a designer coffee at some metrosexual hangout. Hey, what can I say? I am a fifty-year-old crusty, smelly, opinionated cowboy. However, I wonder if the simple answers are the ones we can easily embrace. So here goes.

I think we don't have real friends because we don't *try* to have real friends. Yep, that simple.

Did I raise some eyebrows and blood pressure with that one? "What do you mean, you pig-headed cowboy? I try all the time to make friends!"

"Do you?" I ask.

"Do I? You bet I do! I mean, just last week Bob and I had a beer after work."

That's great. But what did you talk about? Let me guess. If it was anything like most of us, you talked about work, last week's game, and politics. Sound familiar?

Maybe someone wants to tell me, "Hey, pinhead! I go to a men's prayer breakfast every month. What do you say about that?"

Awesome! I used to go to one too—at least until I realized that all we ever talked about was work, last week's game and, you guessed it, politics. Okay, that's not the entire truth. There was the occasional morning when some dude would spill his guts about some emotional garbage he was going through. That's great! The problem was no one, *including me,* ever stepped up to the plate and offered to help the guy get through his stuff. We all shook our heads in agreement; some even muttered a few words like, "Yep, been there, done that." A more spiritual guy may have shared a scripture or two. But then we finished our eggs and went to work. None of us seemed to make the effort to check on the guy and see if he was okay. None of us ever took the time to *try* (there's that word again) to help him along.

Guys, that's *not* friendship! There's no *try* in that. And sadly, I have been as guilty as anyone else.

What was so different when we were boys?

Well, first of all, we were boys. Now we are men! While I realize that in some ways things *are* different now, in the ways that count, they are not. When we were growing up, if one of our friends was having a tough time, say, in school or with a broken family, we were there. We gathered around our buds and took the time to help one another. Yeah, we made each other mad and sometimes even fought. And sometimes we were jerks. But the bottom line was, no matter what, we still were friends.

I get it. Now things are more complicated. Life—with work, a wife, kids, a mortgage, a broken dishwasher, and endless yard work—can be absolutely filled to the max. With all we have going on, how in the world could we ever carve out some time for a meaningful friendship with a guy?

Here is that word again: You gotta *try.* Nothing complicated. No seven-step program to being a better friend. No trips to the local counselor or psychologist. Just plain ol' simple roll up your sleeves, put your stubborn pride aside, and *try.*

I can tell you from experience, it's worth it.

It's not unlike investing hard-earned greenbacks in a savings account. Everything we put into the friendship bank account makes a return on the investment—tenfold. Investing in a real friendship with another guy is one of the most rewarding relationships in a man's life.

LEGENDARY FRIENDS

In the Old Testament, 1 Samuel records the friendship of the young, soon-to-be-king David with Jonathan, the son of the current king, Saul. These two guys knew what it meant to love each other in a manner that was deep, abiding, real, and healthy.

Jonathan, knowing that David was chosen by God to be king, gave up everything. By choice, he loved David enough to offer David his own robe of royalty. David, in return, loved Jonathan as if he were his own brother.

The real key for us to embrace here is that both of them made a concerted effort, sacrificing much, to enrich their friendship. In short, they tried! They each pledged their friendship to the other. Jonathan repeatedly stood in the path of his father's wrath, sheltering his friend. He even sacrificed his crown for the young David. Putting aside the tangled web of life's constant battering, these two noble men chose to love each other enough to fight for their friendship.

The cool thing about it was that the friendship made each a better man. Jonathan became the servant of God's perfect plan for David. David later made a covenant with Jonathan that his family would never be harmed while David was king. This was played out in his offering a place at the king's table to Jonathan's handicapped son, Mephibosheth. The relationship these men cultivated deepened them in ways that would never have happened outside of that friendship. That is the hidden benefit of a powerful friendship between two men.

All through the Bible, men are shown teaming up to accomplish the impossible for God: Moses and Aaron; David and Jonathan; Peter and John; Paul and Timothy; the three leaders of David's indomitable thirty mighty men—Jashobeam, Eleazar, and Abishai. And of course Jesus and His Twelve. We are *better* when we work together. We are at our *best* when we work together in the service of the One who has given us life, Jesus Christ. He is the common ground, the mortar that is foundational in building relationships that go the distance.

I know that my incredible wife, Kim, is stoked when I take the time to get away with guys that I deeply admire and care for and just go be guys. While we enjoy horses, fishing, shooting, war movies, and football games, the real deep and abiding benefit is the *try* we put into one another. Long gone is the keeping-it-superficial with the questions about politics, the local football team, or just what's up. Our time is enriched by the stuff that causes us to go deep, to challenge, to hold each other accountable. That's what makes a friendship.

Whether we're drinking coffee, on horseback, or tying a fly, our conversation sometimes sounds like this:

"Hey, bud, are you surfing the Internet looking for stuff that you shouldn't be looking at?"

"So how are things with your secretary?"

"Are you daily spending time in God's Word, the handbook? Really? So what is God teaching you?"

That's the stuff that matters. That's the life-changing, abiding friendship that goes the distance. That's the filet mignon of friendship while others are still dining on mac and cheese.

Yeah, I get it. Sometimes it's hard to ask those questions for a gazillion different reasons. But frankly, *so what?* Life is too dang short to keep on living alone on some pity-party-filled deserted island. Get over your petty fears and get down to the business of creating lifelong friendships with the guys around you.

THESE ARE THE GOOD OLD DAYS

Let's be frank: those simple days of youth are long gone. That's okay. Quite honestly, I am glad—the time for childish things is over. If you are middle-aged, bored, and still whining about the "good old days," I've got a message for you: get over it! The good old days are happening today. Your life is going by whether you choose to live it or not.

Our lives are consumed with a ton of really good stuff—that's no problem. But the real trick is to carve out time to enrich relationships with the men we admire, men who make us better and are just a kick in the pants to be with.

Men like Randy, my buddy on the steelhead fishing trip...

"Pull your head out, Huck, before you lose him!" Randy called out from behind his video camera as he taped my battle with the steelhead.

"Shut it, you ugly Sasquatch-looking jarhead!" I actually smiled over my shoulder as I reared back once again, fighting the big fish at the end of my line. Jeff chewed on his typical six-dollar cigar (probably one I paid for) and cracked up watching the two of us. "You sound like some crazy old married couple," he said.

Yeah, maybe so, but I was having the time of my life. Here I was in the staggering, matchless beauty of creation, sharing life with two of my best friends. Times like these create a depth of spirit that is unmatched. I felt like a kid again.

With a sweep of his fishnet, Jeff effortlessly scooped up the still-thrashing monarch of the Pacific Northwest. The battle was over. Screaming whoops and hollers that would wake the dead, the three of us exalted in the victory with our hands reaching to the skies together. At our feet lay a textbook, twelve-pound steelhead hen. *Perfect.*

The picture of that day is forever carved in my memory. It was not because of the weather, how fancy the boat was, the food, the cigars, or even the fish. What I won't forget is the time spent with my friends. As the years go by, as gray hair replaces brown, as my body fails, I will always smile at the recollection of that day.

Guys, you don't have to catch a steelhead, climb Mount Denali, raft the Colorado River, or kill an elk in the Rockies to capture what I am talking about here. While good, these things are only the means to creating memories with friends. They are not the reason for friendship.

Maybe it's a sandlot softball game on some sunny Saturday, a living room full of friends around the Super Bowl, building a carport for an elderly neighbor, or a short-term missions trip with Habitat for Humanity. It doesn't matter. The important thing is to just *try.*

I challenge you to be the one who instigates a weekly card game, a car project, a bowling team, a yearly fishing derby—*all* in an effort to bring friends together for what matters. *Life!* The little boy in all of us is long gone. That's okay. But how about living life as the man God has made you to be?

The band of brothers we all seek is just down the road, at church, or across town.

(Written for Goddy, Worm, Hollywood, and Doc.)

10

The Test

It is October. The stinging chill in the air heralds the arrival of the fall season. Very soon, in the weeks to come, my comfortable mountain perch will be blanketed in nature's icy white.

The rugged peaks of the North Cascades spread out before me like the jagged backs of prehistoric dinosaurs. Gazing skyward, my vision fills with the tapestry of creation. Far above, like huge bundles of freshly picked cotton, cumulous clouds rumble through the endless expanse of blue. Announcing an oncoming storm, these dancers of the sky gather in the eternal expression of submission and honor to their Creator. Some reach high into the stratosphere; others skirt the tops of soaring granite peaks that stretch endlessly before me.

Above are the creatures of the sky...below, the earthbound ones. Some three thousand or so feet below me, a small creek winds its way through Fisher Creek basin. Like a brilliant silver ribbon of glass, the water has for eons carved the great chasm through the solid rock walls. Grassy meadows, pine trees, and blood red vine maples cover the great gorge. The picture is beyond words.

Kim silently, with her eyes closed, basks in the fleeting warmth of the afternoon sun. Chloe and Sevi, our Queensland blue heelers, also enjoy a quiet moment, both asleep at her side.

For hours we had worked our way up the ancient North Cascade trail known as "Easy Pass." Almost an oxymoron, there is nothing easy about this popular trekking destination deep in the Washington wilderness. Once used by explorers, miners, and travelers, the Easy Pass trail was, in the late 1800s, the simplest way to get over one of hundreds of arduous mountain passes that fill this place we have come to enjoy.

Today, we simply enjoyed the hike. The steep ascent challenges the hiker to climb some twenty-eight hundred vertical feet to reach the breathtaking summit. We had climbed this route many times, each journey filled with remarkable scenery, inclement weather, and varied wildlife.

As I finish my second peanut butter and jelly sandwich, I am taken by the simple beauty, presence, and grace of my life partner. As she, with eyes closed, drinks in the cool mountain air, I am most thankful…thankful to the Lord of all that we have made it. I am not talking about the climb. That was easy. Well, in the bigger scheme of things, it was. This day, life is good.

As I recall the events of time gone by, memories not so good rise to the surface. More than a decade

past, our lives could have taken a turn we both would
have deeply regretted. What was then could have
easily destroyed what was to come. In each of us the
enemy had taken a foothold.

We were near divorce.

I guess, like so many couples, our story had followed the familiar,
well-worn path of "meet, date, fall in love, marry."

I met Kim in 1979 in Palo Cedro, California, where I was working at a small grocery store. My work schedule included Sundays.
She always came in after church, dressed in her Sunday best. Reli-
giously, she purchased a green apple, a pack of blue Trident gum, and
a diet soda. At her every visit I struggled nervously to simply share a
brief hello, exchange small talk, and watch her leave with her friends.
She took my breath away.

After weeks of this, I finally summoned the courage to ask Kim
for her phone number, only to set it aside and, out of shyness, not call
her for weeks. What I didn't know was that she was coming into the
store to, well, meet me.

On a warm Sunday afternoon, several weeks later, I called. Our
first date was to church. After our second, we knew we would spend
our lives together.

Two years later, we married.

I suppose, as do all young couples venturing out to see what God
has for them, we expected life to be grand. And it was. We laughed,
played, worked tirelessly, and served Jesus wherever we felt Him lead.
And we were always broke. Life revolved around working several
jobs, mac and cheese, and playing Hearts by the light of a single 60-
watt bulb.

Our bed was on the floor with the bugs. Our fancy yard-sale color television had only one color...green. That old RCA made every show look like *M.A.S.H.* Kim drove an old VW; I had the pickup. Life was a constant adventure.

As I recall those early years, I am convinced that Satan is as patient as he is cunning. And he doesn't care whether you are a famous athlete or a working-stiff average Joe—his passion is ruining lives. We go along our merry way while the enemy of our souls quietly— often without our awareness—executes his destructive plan. For him, an attack years in the making is just fine.

While everything about our young life seemed healthy, the rotting cancer of sin, even what seemed to be private sin, was eating away at the core of who we were. Slowly, ever so slowly, the viral infection of compromise was replacing the steadfast truth of God's perfect plan for us. Our relationship began to disintegrate right before our eyes.

THE RESPONSIBLE HUSBAND

The marriage relationship between a husband and a wife is an earthly image of the church and Christ. Ephesians 5:32 says, "This is a great mystery, but [marriage] is an illustration of the way Christ and the church are one." Within the context of marriage, no failure in a relationship is one-sided. It always takes two. However, I strongly believe that the health of a marriage is directly related to the spiritual health and leadership of the husband, the "pastor" of the home. When things go south, more often than not, it is because we husbands have failed to embrace our role in the manner God intended.

I suppose that statement raises a few eyebrows. Sorry, guys, but in my mind the buck stops with us. When you truly search the heart of God and honestly look deep within yourself, I think you will agree: we are the leader of our home. As husband and father, we are to take on the mantle of authority over and responsibility for our family.

We Christian men all love the whole "submit to me" thing. You and I have heard it—or said it: "I am the man! You should submit to my every wish! I am the lord of my castle. Blah, blah, blah." We *love* that part. But we're not so enthusiastic about being submitted fully to Christ. We internally strut around, beating our chest in some brazen attempt to appear tough and in control. We like to take credit for the victories at home, but we tend to blame everyone else for the failures.

When life is good, the bills are paid, the kids are getting good grades, and our bride is grinning from ear to ear, well, it's because we are the consummate husband. But when life stinks, we blame the job, the economy, the kids, even our wife. We never choose to blame the one in leadership—ourselves. Isn't that interesting? At work, when the company is failing, who do we accuse? *The boss.* When the church is struggling, in trouble, who then? *The pastor.* Heaven forbid we look in the mirror when our family is disintegrating.

We work hard to embrace all the macho crap about making the money, buying the toys, having the good job. But what we average Joes need most is to be a man after God's heart.

The Bible is very clear about what belongs on the throne of our heart: His name is Jesus. We are created by Him, for Him. Our life has been bought with a price. That price was Christ's precious blood. If we say we are believers—Christians—but then choose to serve other gods, we set ourselves up for failure, even the potential loss of a mate. That was my story.

Life was all about me, and for years I expected Kim to meet my every need. She, by my choice, was on the throne of my heart. The core of who and what I was revolved around her. I guess in some twisted way I made Kim the lord of my life. I suppose some would have thought my attitudes and behavior were noble: "Oh, how sweet! Troy is such a devoted husband. He is so attentive and kind to her."

No, the truth was that I followed Kim around like some lovesick puppy. I was her yes-man. Without my ever providing an original thought or act of leadership, we struggled year after year. Kim was my self-appointed leader. She assumed the role of pastor of our home.

Sure, I worked hard at my job. I came home every night... mowed the grass...fixed the deck...tuned up the car...volunteered at church. In the world's eyes, I was a good husband, a nice guy. Sadly, though, behind the facade of this seemingly normal marriage, an infection was growing. God never intended for a wife to lead the family. That's a man's job. My intentional decision to step aside where it counted—in the spiritual headship of our marriage—set in motion a cascading degeneration that nearly cost us everything.

Kim was not meant to be Christ in my life. Deep within me and in all men (women too) are empty holes that only He can fill. We sometimes put all our personal stock in the way our wife responds to us. We expect her, an imperfect being, to be perfect in meeting our every need and wish.

I didn't realize it, but I was setting Kim up for complete failure. While my wife, my friend, was tireless in attempting to fill the role I put her in, by design she couldn't fill it. Because I was stepping aside, she was forced to take on the full assault of life. I was such a coward. Attending church was important to her, not me. Praying together could have been the very glue that held us together, but I chose to, well, not pray. A 1998 study by the Georgia Family Council found that when couples prayed together at least once a week, only 7 percent ever seriously considered divorce. But among those who never prayed together, 65 percent had seriously considered divorce.

Even in simple daily decision making, I chose to thrust Kim into the arena of the leadership of our home. My childish attitude was, "Hey, I make the money around here, sort of. The rest is up to her!"

What a poor excuse for a man I was.

As men we were created to be the covering for our families—the ones who shelter all those under our care from the storms of life. But that's the easy part. It's leading our loved ones to the foot of the cross that makes us men. Get your family to church. Better yet, be the pastor of your own home. Here is a novel one: *pray* with your family. Not just the casual "Hey, God, thanks for the grub!" I mean, do business with Jesus *with* your family.

Are you studying and meditating on God's Word every day? Yes, friend, *every* day! Do your kids, when they rise, see their father spending time with the Father? Or is the *New York Times,* the local news rag, or some ESPN talk show more important? Why should we fill our minds with worthless drivel instead of the priceless, powerful, life-changing Word of God?

I confess—I did *none* of this in the early years of our marriage. I lived in Kim's shadow, and by doing so, I piled expectations on her that she could never meet, even though she tried valiantly.

I loaded my needs for my self-worth, passion, joy, wisdom, and security onto her unqualified shoulders. What was meant for God, she tried to bear. When she failed, I began to seek fulfillment elsewhere.

I suppose, as men, we often do that. We look hard at everything around us in our feeble efforts to find meaning and contentment in places that God never intended. Maybe it is within our work? That's where I looked. Working hard—that seems a noble quality. But I put my career ahead of both God and Kim. Although I was successful, fulfillment eluded me. The corner office was not enough. The big annual bonus disappeared in paying bills and taxes. My trail of failure was cut by selfishness, insecurity, and pride.

Sadly, in recent years, I have seen many men seek a more sinister path. With the arrival of the Internet, dabbling with easily available Web sites—ones from the shadows—became an elixir many men find hard to ignore. It's too easy to reach those edgy and dark sites.

What starts with a quick flyby peek every now and then becomes an almost daily crawl into darkness. These infectious, mind-numbing traps begin the insidious contamination of a man's very soul.

My friend, the lure of what can be seen on the computer screen is an infection leading unto death. Trust me—it will rot your core. I have seen it happen time and time again to men. When they walk that well-traveled superhighway of lust, their honor, self-respect, integrity, and resolve are all exchanged for some putrid excuse of manhood. Sadly, this depraved expressway to hell seldom includes just visual stimulation. Often what a man sees turns into what he does. He begins to compromise in every area of his life. Sinning becomes easier. All the while the covenant relationship between himself and the wife God gave him crumbles right in front of his eyes.

On the Brink

My memory of one particular day within this black season is vivid, brutal.

Kim and I had decided to go down to get coffee at the local coffee stand in Tumalo. For weeks we had been struggling. Long gone were the days of laughter, gentleness, and joy. Strife, arguing, and sadness had become the norm. I suppose we had hoped that by taking a short drive and treating ourselves to a hot cup of Joe, we could set aside our struggles for a moment or two.

We were wrong. During the fifteen-minute ride, our light conversation turned into a discussion that soon became a heated argument. After years of seemingly normal day-to-day conflict, our relationship began to spiral into deep trouble. Heated words flew like daggers to the heart. We both spewed vile accusations, hurtful memories, deep regrets. Kim started to cry, the tears soon streaming down her cheeks. My anger burned as I vehemently blamed her for all our failings. Like a rage-infused charging bull, I lashed out at the woman I love.

How can a man be so cruel? Only a few years earlier I had promised before God to love and cherish Kim. How did I get from vowing to cover and care for her to being so selfish and calloused, my selfish desires waging war against what was real and true?

We fought all the way back to the ranch. Pulling into the driveway, I stopped the truck at the bottom of the small hill our house sits on. In an explosion of emotion, Kim launched her final attempt to shake loose the chains of hell around both of us. My response was the same...loud, explosive, and self-righteous. With a flood of passion, she flung open the truck door, looked at me with eyes wet with emotion, and screamed, "You need to leave!" Slamming the door, she backed away two steps and flung her coffee against the window. She staggered up the hill, arms held tightly to her side, her body wracked with sobs.

"Fine!" was my condescending, prideful response. With a quick turn of the wheel, I spun my old Dodge around and headed toward the gate, never intending to return again to the small ranch we had built together. With one final look in the rearview mirror, I pulled out of our gravel drive. Through the black smoke pouring from the Cummins diesel engine of my truck, our mailbox disappeared from view.

It was over.

The enemy had won. Sin ruled the day. Instead of standing in the truth that is Jesus Christ, I had chosen the easy way out—the well-traveled highway of the self-absorbed quitter. Long gone from my life were words like *honor, integrity,* and *covenant.* I had replaced them with *complacency, compromise,* and *conciliation.*

The high desert near our ranch drew me. Snow was now falling, and as I sped east for miles, I could almost hear the enemy laughing at me: "You are such a loser. You will never amount to anything. You can do better than her. She never loved you anyway. You will find someone else. Get a divorce; *everyone else does!*"

In that second...the deceiver lost.

In the cab of that roaring red dually, I heard myself call out to the One who had made me. "Jesus...help me!" I cried. "Please, Father...I need You. *I don't want to be like everyone else.* I don't want to be some statistic, another marriage failure. What in the world has happened to us? I don't want to be a loser...a quitter."

As if it were yesterday, I remember the exact place I turned off the highway. The small BLM dirt road meandered over an antiquated cattle guard and then off into the desert. After a mile or so, I stopped, turned off the engine, and wept. Years of sorrow, sin, and junk poured out of my heart and down my face. At times I could barely breathe. For what seemed like hours, the crust of my hardened heart broke under the weight of my Savior's love.

What a patient God we serve. For years, while I had run away from His side, He had been waiting for me. In a breath, He was there. I cried out; He answered. What is it about our God that He would lower Himself to meet with a broken, battered, selfish, prideful man...in the cab of an old Dodge pickup? That cold, snowy day in November, the King of kings put His arms around what was left of me...and the healing began.

I couldn't get home fast enough.

Questions filled my mind as I neared our driveway. Would Kim still insist I leave? Would she be packing her bags? Would her broken heart ever heal? Could we ever start again?

Turning the bend at the top of our driveway, I had my questions answered.

Kim had heard the rumble of my truck. Leaving the house, she chose to meet me at the bottom of our outdoor stairs, right by the garage. Her tender green eyes said it all. With a faint smile and soft voice, she said, "I thought I would never see you again."

Time stood still. Two tired, damaged, broken people embraced. Two people said together, "We will not quit. We will not give up."

With the whisper of falling snow forming our cathedral of forgiveness, we let go of what was and began the slow process of building what was to come. We said yes to our Creator, yes to our promise given each other years before.

I think often of the words in Psalm 51. King David had sinned. His life was on a downward spiral set in motion by his choices. God was not the reason for his failure; he was, and he knew it. He wrote, "Against you, and you alone, have I sinned" (verse 4). David, the man after God's own heart, had become an adulterer and a murderer. While his sin had cost the life of Uriah and the honor of Bathsheba, David's sin ultimately was against God. We so easily forget that.

The truth is, friend, *all* of us will one day stand before our Creator and be held accountable for how we have lived our lives. Our wives won't be there with us. Our children either. Nor friends, family, relatives. We will be alone. David got that. He knew his sin was against God and God alone. So was mine.

As the sun slips deep in the western sky, Kim and I gather our backpacks, call the dogs, and head down the trail. Our hike up Easy Pass is ending. Kim, with a gentle smile and the soft glow of twilight on her face, whispers quietly, "This was a perfect day."

I agree.

We could easily have given up. We chose not to. Now, many years later, I am in awe of the Father's provision. He truly does "restore to you the years that the locusts hath eaten" (Joel 2:25, KJV).

While not perfect—no relationship is—our love for each other has matured and our marriage has healed. I cannot imagine life without Kim. She is the love of my youth, the joy of my existence, my very best friend.

What more could an average Joe—or any Joe for that matter—ask for?

11

The Deep

WITH A GRIN AND A QUICK THUMBS-UP, Kelsie nodded that she was ready.

The early morning sky overpowered the waning darkness of the dying night as the sun rose above the horizon. Gentle early morning warmth greeted us through the lee of West Maui and Mount Haleakala. It was another perfect day in Hawaii.

Our trip by boat from Kihei to our dive site took only minutes. Now, nearly three miles offshore, it was time to get wet. Time to go from the familiar into the unknown.

As humans we thrive in the world God created for us, the world above the waves. The deep blue, on the other hand, while beautiful, can be hostile and unforgiving. We have lungs, not gills. No, we are not Aquaman or Kevin Costner in *Waterworld*, and we for sure are not like that guy in *The Abyss*, the one who inhaled and exhaled the pink, special juju water. Come on, we were meant to breathe good ol' polluted oxygen!

And yet, for some of us, the lure of the unknown is an elixir that we are compelled to drink. Scuba-diving is that enticing swill for me. Growing up, I was mesmerized by tales of adventure under the sea. Every Sunday evening our family gathered around the television and watched in awe as Jacques Cousteau traveled the world to bring us *The Undersea World of Jacques Cousteau*. How many thousands of boys like me grew up dreaming of stepping off the dive platform of Cousteau's boat *Calypso* and searching the great expanse of the unknown—the world under the waves.

Some thirty years later, here I was in the deep, cobalt blue of the Pacific Ocean as it gently cradled the boat beneath my feet.

This was Kelsie's first dive. For years she had dreamed of learning how to scuba-dive. As I methodically checked my gear, I thought about how many years it had been since Kelsie, that small, rebellious, curly haired twelve-year-old, had first walked up the driveway of our home and ministry, Crystal Peaks Youth Ranch. Now twenty-two, she had become like a daughter to me and was one of my dearest friends. In the last year, Kelsie had saved her money, taken the classes, and passed her exam. The open-water diver certification on her dive log said it all. She was a scuba diver.

For months she had looked forward to this day. We had both planned and prepared for our adventure together, "father" and "daughter" scuba-diving in the open ocean. As I looked across the dive boat at her, the emotions I felt must have been what a father feels when he spends time with his children.

Kim and I have, by choice, never had kids of our own. We had many long conversations about God's perfect plan for our lives. Late into countless nights we wrestled with starting a family or fully devoting ourselves to the ministry He'd given us. We chose the ministry.

I admit, there have been times when we both questioned whether or not we have done the right thing. Have we missed a blessing, a treasured gift that the Giver of life wanted to share with us? A wiser person than me—which means just about everyone—once shared with Kim, "While you may not be a mother to one or two of your own, you are mom to the hundreds that God has shared with you over the years." So even though Kelsie is not my biological child—she has wonderful parents who deeply love her—at this moment, I think I sensed the love a father must feel for his daughter.

While I have the opportunity, I want to say something to anyone reading this who is a father: Dads, never forget the life-changing power you hold within your grasp. *Your daughters need you!* Nothing in this world is more important than time with your kids, especially your daughters. We get so caught up in the things we *think* are important. I know... You have heard this a thousand times. Well, you are going to hear it again! Your little girls need you. If they don't find love in you, they will look for it elsewhere. Sadly, many search for it in the places we never want them to look.

Our world would radically change for the better if more fathers would step up to the plate and love their daughters as they should. *You* should be their first date. *You* should tell them about boys and how their minds think, the little grubby horn dogs. Dance with them in the living room. Take them to Cold Stone for an ice cream *more than once. You* should be the one who gives them complete confidence that you love them no matter what. Instead of being the big, tough guy at the door with a baseball bat, waiting for her first date to walk up and ring the bell, how much better to have a relationship with your little girl that gives her confidence and security. May she *know* that no matter what her date tells her, her daddy loves her without question. May she *know* with complete certainty that her father is crazy about her and would do whatever it takes to protect and cherish her.

Okay, off my soap box.

PANIC DOWN UNDER

Back to the boat in Hawaii...

With our gear passing its final safety check, we grinned and prepared to step off the dive platform into the deep blue. As we both signaled we were good to go, the dive master gave us the go-ahead, and we stepped off into the temperate Pacific.

The warm salt water rushed in to fill our wet suits. We had finally made it. The sea greeted us with the gentle rise and fall of calm two- to three-foot waves. Donning my mask, I looked down. The deep, tranquil, underwater world extended as far as I could see. I felt like I was leaving the world of the known to venture into the timeless chambers of the unknown. As Kelsie and I floated on the surface, we both knew we were going from the environment in which we belonged to one that, while beautiful, can be hostile and threatening.

The dive master's instructions to us were simple: do a quick equipment check, clear your regulator, set your buoyancy compensator to a comfortable descent speed, check the dive computer, and head to the bottom...110 feet below. Because I needed to descend slowly (bad ear from sticking a pencil in it as a kid), we decided to head for the bottom along the dive-flag line. Anchored at the bottom, the dive flag gives divers and the boat crew a fixed reference point to return to in the event of trouble.

With an "okay" signal, Kelsie and I started down. From the noisy, wave-tossed surface, we entered the silent world of the deep. My mind instantly went back thirty-five-plus years to that little boy captivated every Sunday evening by the men of the *Calypso*. I vividly recalled sitting in front of our ancient Magnavox and diving with Jacques deep into the unknown. Now, real fish of all shapes, colors, and sizes surrounded Kelsie and me. Dozens of sergeantfish, angels, moorish idols, parrotfish, and the humuhumunukunukuapuaa— say that one five times fast—all seemed to point the way to the bottom. The water was crystal clear. We could easily see schools of fish and several eels cruising the bottom, over one hundred feet down.

Ten feet...twenty feet...thirty feet... Everything looked good. A quick glance at Kelsie—she seemed fine. Forty feet...fifty feet...

The boat above us seemed an awful long way up. *Is this the right depth?* I wondered. My regulator seemed to be laboring as I breathed. Man, this was a long way down, and I still had sixty feet or so to go. Kelsie, God bless her, was doing somersaults in the water. Like a fish in a pond, she seemed right at home.

Okay, Troy, everything is cool. Remember your training. Just a simple trip to the bottom. Sixty feet…seventy feet… *What was that? What was that shadow?*

The pressure of the water around me increased, and my slow, easy breathing was replaced with panic-infused gulps of air. I couldn't get enough oxygen. My vision blurred. The pounding in my chest was a heart racing out of control. It hit me like a ton of bricks…like a claustrophobic wave closing in on me…

*Panic…*AAAAARRRRRGGGGGHHHHH!

My brain shifted its attention from the peaceful quiet of the moment to sheer and complete terror. My breathing became desperate. Like a locomotive out of control, I could feel myself losing my sensibilities. *AIR…I can't get enough air.* I frantically reached for my dive computer, hoping I had air. It read almost full. *What? I felt like I was out!*

My survival instincts kicked into high gear. *Swim for the surface, you fool! You are* NOT *going to survive. You can't do this. Oh, crap, what if my regulator is fouled? What if my mask falls off? What if I can't make it back to the surface?* My thoughts spun out of control. *You are going to die here, you idiot!* I struggled to regain composure. I looked up and the boat seemed miles away. *Did I go too deep? Am I caught in a strong current? Great, they will probably find me somewhere off the coast of Russia!*

Grabbing the anchor rope I started hauling my butt back to the surface. Fifty feet… Forty-five feet…

Stop! Make it stop! my Neolithic brain screams.

Almost in an instant, the mental assault stopped. Without warning, clear vision returned. Breathing slowed. Heartbeat eased. Everything cleared.

So…why did I react this way? Was I bitten by a shark? Did a giant octopus pull my leg off? Did a whale swim by and thump me on the head? Did Captain Nemo cruise by and steal my marbles? No, *nothing* happened. No ominous sea creature swam from the deep to steal my air. I was not bitten by Jaws. The sea was quiet. The sun was creating a beautiful dance of light on the bottom sixty feet down. Nothing happened.

As I started my emergency ascent, I looked at Kelsie and she seemed fine, the little twerp. In fact, she was grinning from ear to ear. Her breathing looked normal, and like a leaf falling to the ground, she was gently continuing her effortless trip to the bottom. Seeing my frantic look as I hauled myself to the surface, she must have wondered what the heck I was doing.

My mind still raced: *Wait! I'm the one with all the dives in my dive book. I'm the one who's been diving since before she was born. I mean, I'm the guy, the man here… She is just a kid… On her first dive, she's making me look like an idiot. Okay, I'm making myself look like an idiot.*

After rising ten or so feet up the anchor line, I stopped my panicked surge for the surface—I'm not sure why. I would like to say it was courage, nerve, or plain old guts. Sadly it was probably pure, unadulterated, stubborn pride. I didn't want to be left behind, outdone by…a girl! At forty-five feet from the surface, I stopped.

Kelsie, several feet below me, motioned to see if I was all right.

Sheepishly, with a very embarrassed "okay" signal, I motioned yes.

What had happened? What caused me to travel the short road from controlled sanity to uncontrolled panic? How did I go from being comfortable with my situation to absolutely scattering my marbles, to losing touch with my surroundings and the truth of what was going on?

The shadow of the boat above gently rocked back and forth across the ocean bottom. The sun streamed into the water in shafts of gold. Nothing had changed. From the moment I'd left the dive platform to now, nothing was different, nothing except maybe me.

In that instant I became keenly aware that as men we struggle with stuff that we should not contend with. Each day we rise before the dawn. After a shower and a shave, we shuffle our tired feet to the kitchen for a morning wake-up call of coffee and the newspaper. Precious moments are spent with wife and kids. Then, like lemmings, we trudge off to a job that we might dislike. We spend eight to ten hours shuffling papers, building broomsticks, or selling furniture. We may spend life-numbing hours fighting traffic, only to come home to screaming kids and a worn-out wife. We do this day after day after day, unaware of a coming catastrophe. We are in the middle of stuff we have done for years, in the middle of a scuba-dive, and at fifty feet in a calm sea, something hits us from out of the blue and WHAM! Life takes a turn for the worse and we panic.

Out of the Blue

Have you been there? Life was just truckin' along and—crack!—out of the blue, you got hit by a lightning bolt that caused you to run screaming to your momma. Maybe it was a tax audit, a bad medical report, a child caught with drugs, a companywide layoff, or—who knows? We just know that we panicked. We responded like little children and ran for cover into alcohol, work, an affair, or whatever.

In the book of 1 Samuel, the Bible tells an incredible story about a simple, average guy who, in the face of certain death, did not panic.

He was nothing special. This guy named David was the youngest of eight brothers. Saul, the king at that time, had made huge mistakes with God. Even though Saul had appeared to be perfect king material, a big strapping fellow (not an average Joe) who made the ladies swoon, God had had enough and commissioned the prophet Samuel to choose the next king over Israel from among these eight brothers.

Their dad, Jesse, paraded seven of his sons in front of the prophet, but Samuel took God's warning to not be impressed with any one of them and asked Jesse if he had any more boys. "Well, there is still the youngest," he responded. This mere boy, David, was the runt, the average Joe in the family. He wasn't like his brothers, all fancied up and full of himself. David was a shepherd, and he was out taking care of the family business. While the brothers were doing whatever older brothers do—chasing girls, waxing dad's chariot, hanging out at the local burger joint—David was tending to smelly, stubborn sheep.

Now that's a career we would all grow up wanting, right? Hardly. In those days, the lowly shepherd job was not what young boys dreamed about. Back then the popular boyhood dreams probably included captain of the guard, chariot driver, or palace advisor to the king. I am quite confident that shepherd was not a highly sought-after vocation, yet David, the average Joe, had the job.

Samuel saw David and anointed him the next king of Israel. But the throne was not available yet, so David went back out into the field to herd sheep. Just like you and me, he set the alarm for 0-dark-thirty, brewed the coffee, and got back to doing his job. Kings don't do that; average Joes do!

All seemed to be going well for our young anointed ruler and then...BAM! Out of the blue came the reason for panic. At nine feet tall, Goliath was a man to be reckoned with. He was the best of the best. The champion of the Philistine army. The Rock'em Sock'em Robot of the day. David was to be king, but in his way stood a mountain of a man: Goliath.

You know the story. David confronted Goliath. Goliath cursed

David and David's God. David got ticked off, picked up a few rocks, slung one at Goliath, and hit him in the noggin. The big dude fell, David killed him, and everyone partied with David.

Well, the story goes that way, sort of, but I am convinced—if we read it like a children's bedtime story—we miss several of the strongest life lessons we average Joes can learn from our pal David.

History records that Goliath and David squared off in the Valley of Elah. On one side was the giant. His armor alone weighed over 125 pounds. David, on the other hand, was a teenage boy—"ruddy and handsome, with pleasant eyes" (1 Samuel 16:12). What do you suppose Goliath's description was—scarred, scraggly beard, bad teeth? This scene was so much more than a benign deep-water scuba-dive in the warm Pacific. This was a time for panic, a life-or-death situation.

Have you ever felt that way? I have. Just when you think you have everything under control, here it comes: another giant. Sadly, more often than not, I panic instead of standing on the promises of Jesus Christ. I choose to run and hide instead of remembering that the battle is His, not mine. Like King Jehoshaphat, when faced with insurmountable odds, I must remember that the battle belongs to the Lord: "This is what the LORD says: Do not be afraid! Don't be discouraged by this mighty army, for the battle is not yours, but God's" (2 Chronicles 20:15).

David could have panicked, but he didn't. In the face of certain death, David stood his ground. He chose to mock the giant instead of cowering before him. David chose to run to the fight instead of waiting for the fight to come to him. David used the tools—the sling and the stones—that he was familiar with to defeat his enemy. In time of trouble, David called on the name of Almighty God; he relied not on his own strength, but on his Maker's. David stood in the fire of adversity and fought.

Will you? Will I?

Facing Fear

Back to my dive...

As I worked to gather my wits, I realized that choosing to panic would not improve my situation. I was still forty-five feet below the surface. The day was as beautiful as when I'd entered the water. Kelsie was still gently sinking to the seafloor. In that instant, I had a choice: I could either chicken out and give way to my stupid fears, or see the giant for what it was—not a giant at all. After a deep breath and a quick equipment check, I chose to resume my journey to the bottom.

In that moment, that microsecond when we all make the decision to "cowboy up," I chose to seek what was real, to see the situation for what it was, and like fog evaporating in the sun, the panic went away. The "giant" backed down. My fear gently, like the quiet current of the ocean, drifted away. Panic was replaced by peace.

As I reached the sandy bottom, fear was trumped by simplicity and wonder. For a short moment I sat on the soft, white sand and reveled in the perfect world around me. With flawless clarity, I could see hundreds of garden eels, schools of moorish idols, sergeantfish, parrotfish, and others swimming lazily by. It was like lounging inside a huge aquarium.

Our dive plan took us from the gentle white sands of the middle of Molokini Crater at one hundred-plus feet to the sloping walls of coral that formed the outer reef of this extinct volcano. For over thirty minutes our small group of adventurers cruised the crystal-clear water surrounding the crater. Whitetip reef sharks rose from the depths below to see what was swimming just above. While harmless, they always add excitement to every dive.

Kelsie seemed at home in the deep. I traveled the lower part of the reef in depths up to 135 feet. Kelsie effortlessly glided above, searching the grottos and reefs that revealed the violent history of the crater. Once used as target practice for passing World War II fighter planes, Molokini Crater is now a marine sanctuary, set aside for future generations to enjoy.

When our air tanks were nearly exhausted, Kelsie and I ascended. At fifteen feet we made a short stop to clear any built-up nitrogen or gas bubbles in our blood. Called a decompression stop, this was critical to assure we would not experience the ravages of the bends or caisson disease. At this depth, we cruised out into the endless blue. As if suspended in space, we held there for a few short minutes, watching schools of game fish in the distance, most likely huge yellowfin tuna. The Bible teaches that all creation shouts the glory of the Lord. Suspended in the Pacific Ocean with three hundred feet of water below, a huge volcano off to one side, and schools of yellowfin tuna on the other, I am certain the Lord and Kelsie could hear me yee-hawing through my regulator.

We had the time of our lives.

Each and every day we choose whether or not to fight in the face of adversity. As men we encounter numerous Goliaths standing in our way. You have yours and I have mine. We don't have the choice as to whether or not trouble will find us. Trust me, the giants will look us up. However, we do have the choice, when adversity rears its insidious head, to panic or not. We can choose, in the face of the hurricane, to stand in the strength of the One who allowed the storm.

It is easy, in the face of certain struggles, maybe even death, to panic. The hurricanes of life will rage. Crises will come. The true test of the man, the average Joe, is his response within the storm. Will you, will I, cower before the oncoming giant, or will we stand in the strength of Jesus Christ? Will you and I trust in the One who has already won the battle?

I love the movie *True Grit*. In one of the final scenes, John Wayne—a.k.a. Rooster Cogburn—with the reins in his teeth, horse at a full gallop, and guns blazing, yells out to the bad guys: "Fill your hands, you son of a @#&%!"

In that moment, Cogburn—an average, old, fat guy—chooses not to panic in the face of certain death but to meet his challenge head-on.

So should we.

12

The Boy

THE CAUSE OF THE DEADLIEST TSUNAMI in history, the enormous Indian Ocean earthquake of 2004, was the beginning of one of the greatest natural disasters modern man has ever seen.

On December 26, with power equal to twenty-three thousand Hiroshima-type atomic bombs, giant forces deep within the earth shook violently, with the epicenter of the quake registering an astonishing 9.0 on the Richter scale. Trillions of tons of seafloor were instantly displaced, causing a catastrophic tsunami that killed over 150,000 people and left millions homeless. Reports came in from all over the world of waves fifty feet high. Video footage from vacationing tourists captured tsunami surges that washed away entire towns, beachfront resorts, villages, and even trains.

On Sunday, December 29, three days after the tsunami, our pastor was finishing his sermon when, without warning, he stopped. With his eyes filling with tears and his voice shaking, Mike said in a near whisper, "We must do something. There are hundreds of thousands in trouble. We can't just sit here and do nothing. We must reach out to these people."

Unknown to me then, on that same day thirteen thousand miles from our little church, a young Sri Lankan boy named Tonaj and his father were digging a hole to bury Tonaj's mother and his only two siblings. The tsunami that had devastated Tonaj's home in the small village of Hikkaduwa had left its heartbreaking fingerprint on his life and thousands like him.

As the church service ended, several of the men who attend our fellowship met Pastor Mike at the back of the sanctuary. There was urgency in the air, and like a moth to a flame, I felt myself drawn to these guys. As I walked toward them, I assured Kim that I just wanted to check it out. She smiled as only she can and gently squeezed my hand. The look in her eyes was clear: you must go.

In a matter of days our team was chosen. We decided that Habitat for Humanity was our best choice as an organization to serve with. They had a new program called First Builder. In simple terms, we would assemble a strike team made up of eight builders, a medic, and a pastor. We would go into one of the worse-hit areas, one in urgent need of help. Our Habitat liaison informed us we were to travel light and expect the unexpected.

On March 9, 2005, on a perfect, early-spring morning in central Oregon, each team member arrived at the church with a sense of purpose and adventure. We were going to do something to help tsunami victims. After many hugs, handshakes, and prayers, our church family cheered as our small, ragtag team pulled out of the drive. After a few long days of travel we would arrive somewhere in the southern reaches of India.

At least that was what we thought.

We had made all the necessary arrangements. After spending the first night in San Francisco, we were scheduled to finalize our documentation with the Indian government at ten o'clock the next morning, followed by a good lunch, and then prepare to board our flight that evening. Sound simple? Well, it did in my little average Joe world.

At 11:30 a.m. we walked out of the Indian consulate with a big fat NO written across all our travel documents. The words still rang in our ears: "We know you guys are not who you say you are, and we don't want you in our country." Those words sank deep in each of our boyish hearts. We each had thoughts like: *Yeah, but we are here to help you. Don't you get the bigger picture? We raised money, made plans, bought tickets, even purchased gifts for the village—and you don't want us to come? I mean, come on, little person behind the counter! We are coming to help you! We are* Americans. *This is what we do!*

Standing in the parking lot of the Indian consulate that spring day, we were dumbstruck and directionless. Like a bunch of kids lost in the woods, maybe even like a bunch of sheep without a shepherd, there we stood, not knowing which way to turn.

I called Kim to share the news. Her response was bright, quick, and wise. "You are water in God's hands," she said. "Allow Him to pour you out wherever *He* chooses."

Wives can be so incredibly wise. We guys get so full of ourselves, rampaging on like bulls out of control. I thank God every day that I have Kim to keep me from running headlong into stupidity, arrogance, and disaster.

I gathered the team in a circle, shared Kim's message, and asked if we could pray that God would pour us out wherever He wanted us to go. So, in that consulate parking lot, ten thickheaded knuckle-draggers gathered in a circle and prayed to our King, asking that we be like water in His hands, ready for pouring.

Our God is unstoppable. With a few short phone calls to Habitat, our visas were reissued, and our plane reservations miraculously rerouted. Our old plans were abandoned; God's plans took shape. That evening we boarded a Singapore Airlines flight bound for Sri Lanka.

The water was being poured out, just into a different bucket than we'd planned.

Helpless Without God

It was two in the morning, fifty-four exhausting hours later, when our final flight touched down on what seemed like a gravel, pothole-filled runway in Colombo, the capital of Sri Lanka. After another day of getting the details of our assignment in order, we were on our way to the small coastal village of Hikkaduwa.

Ravaged by the tsunami, Hikkaduwa had been featured in video footage shown on newscasts around the globe. Railroad tracks were seen ripped from the ground and twisted into odd shapes, and train cars had been tossed like children's toys. The loss of human life was staggering. Even though we arrived three months after the disaster, the overwhelming stench of death still hung in the tepid air. Small mountains of crushed building materials, uprooted palm trees, battered boats and cars, and rotting fish were piled as far as the eye could see.

We spoke very little as our rickety old bus rumbled into the tattered remains of the village. How in the world could we ever make a difference? What could a bunch of redneck Oregonians do to help after a catastrophe of this magnitude? As we drove in the quiet, some prayed, some stared in awe, some even wept. Our task was beyond our comprehension.

It was in that moment that I realized I could do nothing outside the strength and wisdom of my Creator. The Bible speaks of how we are but dust, of how our life is but a wisp of time. What is man that he thinks he can accomplish anything outside the will of God? I wonder if Moses felt this way, leading over a million people through the desert? Or Gideon, as the Lord chose him to fight a battle with seemingly insurmountable odds. I felt extremely small. What could an average Joe do that would make a difference in such extreme destruction?

The enormity of what we were attempting to accomplish was

coming into focus. I still remember the rising doubt and feelings of absolute helplessness as the team exited the bus and simply stared in disbelief at our surroundings. I could only imagine how, months ago, this place had teemed with life. In my mind's eye I could see children playing among the palm trees, mothers hauling water from the village well, and fishermen bringing in the day's catch from the ocean. There would have been huts, gardens, and small businesses lining the road along the coast. This little village was once a place for tourists to come and enjoy the sun, surf in the sea, and shop for semi-precious stones, spices, batik, tea, and coconuts.

This was not what we saw. Nothing was left standing. Mountainous piles of twisted wood, shrubs, and garbage bore testimony to the ferocity of the waves that had leveled entire forests of teak, satin wood, ebony, and palm.

The next twenty-four hours were a blur of activity. Contact was made with a Habitat representative. Language barriers were overcome, materials started to flow into the village, and the honor of building a home for a Sri Lankan family was given to our team and—a welcome surprise—a First Builder team from the Netherlands.

For the next ten days, our two groups worked tirelessly in the sweltering Sri Lankan sun. At six o'clock each morning, we rose from our mosquito net–covered bunks to the warm greeting of our Sri Lankan hosts. They were incredible, serving us hot tea, toast, and eggs daily for breakfast. By 7:00 our Dutch counterparts and Team USA were busy building. A great Dutchman named Marco was my partner and has since become my friend.

By the end of the third day, homes began taking shape. Little 12 by 12 foot concrete huts arose out of the rubbish. Homeless families started to dream that they would soon sleep in houses and the children would have a roof over their heads.

As each day ended, I would pack up my gear, skip the van ride to town, and instead walk the mile or so back to our camp. It was my way of unwinding after the labor and, more importantly, to meet villagers along the way. Amid the stinking mountains of rubbish, I was always greeted with smiles from extraordinary children and adults. Warm salutations of "America Number One!" would ring out from grins with teeth white as snow. Despite circumstances that would crush the typical complacent, spoiled American...*like me*... these people chose to rise from the ashes with dignity, purpose, and pure joy.

Meeting the Boy

On the morning of our sixth day, I met the boy. His name was Tonaj.

As usual, the teams converged at the job site at around 7:00 a.m. Work assignments for the day were announced by the Habitat supervisor, a jolly Dutchman. This morning he asked Marco and me to supervise the start of another house. It was to be Tonaj's home.

With the typical gentle Sri Lankan smile, Tonaj greeted Marco and me with a soft handshake and a warm hello. While he looked to be around nine or ten years old, Tonaj was actually sixteen. Years of poor nutrition, unclean water, and struggle had left him smaller than he should have been.

With the crude rock-and-concrete foundation already laid, our group's task was to build the cinder-block-and-mortar walls. As we gathered our materials and tools, it became clear that Tonaj desired to become part of the construction team. No words were spoken, but by his actions it was clear that this young man was ready to do whatever it took to see his home built. Over the next few days, Tonaj outworked us all.

I met Tonaj's father on the seventh day of our stay. A thin, graying man who appeared to be in his seventies, he was only fifty, I later learned. Like Tonaj, the father had been ravaged by years of struggle. He was friendly, charitable, and kind, yet very sad. His eyes revealed the sorrow and pain of losing his wife and children. After shaking hands, he showed me pictures of his wife and family. In the photo, standing next to Tonaj, were his two sisters, young, beautiful, and full of life. Tears filled the old man's eyes as he, in very broken English, shared about the staggering loss of his loved ones. I could only look at him and, through my own tears, say how sorry I was about his loss. Sometimes words are not enough.

Watching him walk back to his small, temporary grass hut, I was overcome with grief…and the desire to get home myself. I so wanted to see Kim, my family, and my friends, but Bend, Oregon, seemed so very far away. Each day is a gift from our Father in heaven, and the company of our loved ones must be cherished, valued, and treasured. We as fathers, friends, and husbands *must* hold our loved ones every day.

Sadly, Tonaj's father would never hold his girls again.

As the hours passed, Tonaj became more and more my friend and partner. Everywhere I went, whether it was to measure a wall, check a level, or mix concrete, Tonaj was at my side. Whatever I needed, he was there to assist. Time and time again I told him, "Good boy! Good boy, Tonaj. You are doing such a good job. Thank you for all the help."

I didn't know how much he understood. He would just smile and get right back to the task at hand. Together we worked side by side in the sun. What a sight we must have been—the big, dorky cowboy next to the small, capable Sri Lankan. In the mornings I would arrive at the site only to find my little friend already mixing concrete, hauling water, or stacking cinder blocks. At the end of each day, I would leave my tool belt behind because Tonaj wanted to clean my tools and make sure they were ready for the next day. My tools had never looked better.

As we walked to the job site together each morning, I would put my hand on Tonaj's tiny shoulder and tell him, "Good work, Tonaj.

Thank you so much for cleaning my tools." His brown eyes sparkled as he looked up at me. Revealing white teeth, he smiled and gently nodded his head.

What an astonishing young man.

As the next to the last day of our project came to an end, the Habitat interpreter, Rosita, pulled me aside. "Tonaj is very fond of you," she shared. "Sri Lankans are usually very wary of Americans and Europeans. For some reason, Tonaj has allowed himself to become very attached to you."

"What do you mean?" I responded.

"By his actions, he is telling everyone that you are his good friend. It is quite an honor that does not happen very often."

Hearing those words, I realized that I, too, had allowed Tonaj to wiggle his way into my guarded heart.

"Good Boy"

Our last day in Hikkaduwa was filled with conflicting emotions. On the one hand, we were all looking forward to getting home, yet we knew there was still so much to do. In ten days we had opened supply lines, initiated communication with the village elders, completed two homes, and started three others that we wished we could finish. Additional Habitat teams would follow to complete the work. But what an incredible feeling it was to know that at least several families now had shelter from the sun and tropical storms in homes we had built.

After lunch it was decided that we would hold a dedication ceremony for a home the teams had just finished. At the ringing of the village bell, everyone gathered around the front doorway of the small concrete-block house. What a picture! There we all stood—men from Holland and America, Sri Lankan villagers, Habitat representatives, and children—shoulder to shoulder in support of one family.

With sunburned faces, blistered hands, and scrapes and bruises, we all joined together, a bunch of smelly average Joes, content in what we'd accomplished.

But Tonaj was missing.

As the short ceremony came to a close, I asked Rosita if she knew where Tonaj was. "He is still working on his house," she responded. "He never left the site."

"Why?"

"Partly, I think, because he wants to finish his home, but more so because he knows you are leaving and he doesn't want you to go."

A lump began to form in my throat.

I found him, concrete trowel in hand, still working on the structure he soon would call home. While he wasn't really qualified to do much when it came to the construction part of the project, as always, every tool was clean, the concrete was mixed, the ground around the site was raked, and stacks of blocks were ready for laying. He was incredible. Without any instruction, Tonaj had worked harder and with more self-direction than most of the men.

That simple "unqualified" boy was the perfect picture of an average Joe. Tonaj was just a boy in an obscure little third world country. However, in looking back over the years, I have come to think of Tonaj as a simple young man with tenacity, passion, and grit. He was and probably will always be an average Joe. Yet deep within the young boy beat the heart of a warrior. Not unlike David, the boy king, Tonaj—although young, small in stature, and simple in nature—faced his struggles head on.

Rounding the corner of his house, I called out, "Tonaj, come here for a moment." His small weathered hands let go of a shovel he was cleaning, and he quickly came to my side. "I need to talk with you."

Kneeling by his side, I thanked him for working so hard, for being such a "good boy." In a simple expression of gratitude, I gave him my baseball cap and tool belt. His eyes sparkled as he accepted my simple—and clumsy—effort at saying good-bye. Looking deeply into my eyes, he thanked me in broken English.

For days he had tirelessly cleaned our tools, one being a large Swiss army knife I'd purchased for the trip. Numerous times Tonaj had carefully opened, examined, and polished that knife's every blade and tool. I reached into my pocket, pulled out the knife, and placed it in his hands. "Good-bye, my friend," I said. His huge brown eyes glassed over as he looked at the knife. With a simple caring gesture, he reached his tiny hand to mine. As men we shook hands; then as friends we embraced.

I will never forget the feeling I had when he squeezed as hard as his little arms could and quietly said to me, "Good boy." While patting me on the back, over and over he whispered, "Good boy."

For days I had struggled with our lack of tangible communication. The language barrier had seemed insurmountable. Over and over I had told him with a smile, "Tonaj, you are a good boy!" He had always grinned, revealing his brilliant white teeth, and quietly went back to work. I had wondered if he knew what I was trying to say. In that final moment with my little friend, I felt he knew exactly what I'd said. His gift to me was to return the favor.

"Good boy."

Letting him go, I turned and headed for the small bus that would start our journey home. On my way Rosita called out for me to come back and see her and Tonaj's father. I dropped what was left of my gear and walked toward her. From a distance, as our eyes met, I knew something was desperately wrong. Rosita's smile was gone, and her eyes were red from emotion. She, through tears, struggled to share what the father had said: "He wants you to take his son."

"What?" I asked.

"He has lost everything. There is nothing left but his son Tonaj. He wants you to take his son home to America with you and adopt him. He wants a better life for his son. He respects you and knows that Tonaj cares deeply for you."

I was staggered by the request. I felt like someone had sucker-punched me in the gut. All that I could muster was "I can't do that, Rosita. Take his son? Are you kidding me? Tonaj is all he has left."

My eyes blurred, wet with emotion, as raw grief and sorrow battled deep within me. I could see in the man's tear-filled eyes that he was deeply serious. I couldn't imagine the strength and compassion it must have taken for that weathered old man to even suggest such a thing. "He needs his son, and his son needs him" was all I could say as I met the gaze of the man standing before me.

"I know," Rosita answered. "All you can do is thank him, honor him by shaking his hand, and tell him that Tonaj is *his* son and needs to be with *his* father."

The man was no taller than possibly five feet and weighed maybe one hundred pounds. Yet in that moment, as I took his ancient-looking, weathered hand, I felt as though I were shaking hands with an antediluvian sage. With his chin set, his eyes clearing, he was a rock. We stood face to face, eye to eye, with hands locked as Rosita shared in his native tongue that I couldn't take and adopt Tonaj. He quietly shook his head in agreement and, with a gentle nod, squeezed my hand, turned away, and made his way to where his last remaining child was working.

My last sight of Tonaj, the good boy, was of him with his eyes closed, locked in the deep embrace of his father.

Take the Son

I learned so much on that trip to Sri Lanka. I ate king coconuts for the first time, laid awake listening as monkeys screamed in the night, sang worship songs and old John Denver tunes with believers—me in English, they in their native tongue—built homes, made friends with average Joes from Holland, and even surfed in the Indian Ocean. Yet, of all the time I spent in that faraway place, it was in those last few minutes, as I stood eye to eye with a wise man, that the magnitude of God's gift became clear: God the Father desires for us to take His Son.

> For God so loved the world that he gave his only Son, so that everyone who believes in him will not perish but have eternal life. (John 3:16)

Gentlemen, if you embrace nothing else within the pages of this book, embrace this: your Creator loves you. He desires only the very best for you. His passion for you is to find yourself within the saving grace of His Son. Life abundant is found in the perfect will of Jesus Christ. The blood of Jesus Christ, shed on the cross of Calvary, is the *only* thing that will set you free. The God of all creation reaches out to you and to me and asks us to take His Son—to bring home with us the saving grace of Jesus Christ.

We are men. We are the gatekeepers to our homes. We do what we do as fathers, sons, employees, employers—whether professional or blue collar. We fuss and muss about, worrying about the smallest things. We let things like bills, broken pipes, expected promotions, and politics consume our lives.

Yet in all that we do and worry about, the single most important life calling is the handshake we have with God the Father when we look into His eyes and say, "Yes, yes, my King. I will take Your Son home with me. I will embrace Him as Lord of my life. I will embrace Him as the King of who I am. I will be the gatekeeper who opens the door for Him to come in and be in *my home,* with *my family.*

He will be *my Lord.*"

13

The Round Pen

GOD-INSPIRED LIFE LESSONS can often be found in the simple...
sometimes even working with a horse in a round pen.

With only a whisper, she quietly passes by, akin to
liquid night, her every movement gently flowing from
my seemingly motionless cues. Like some black
dream phantom, she effortlessly trots fluid circles
around me. Her ancient, deep, and powerful gaze
never leaves mine. She is an extension of my
thoughts, honoring my every wish. At the tiniest
motion of my hand or intention of my eye, she picks
up her pace. A step toward her shoulder as she
passes, and she slows. When I choose to move
toward her hindquarters, her pace quickens. Without
any physical contact, she responds to my silent
commands.

It's electrifying. As I stand in the center of my
round pen, I seem connected to thirteen hundred
pounds of living, breathing, thinking intelligence,
reacting to my every movement, each simple gesture,
and seemingly my every thought. As she passes by
me, her movements, carriage, and demeanor reveal
the story of her Friesian heritage.

Her name is Eclipse.

For a millennium the Friesian horse has been synonymous with great
size, presence, and powerful, animated movement. Always black in
color, its ancestors have captured the thoughts and dreams of poets,
philosophers, and kings. A war-horse bred by ancient nobles of the
Netherlands, the Friesian's sole purpose was battle. History records
campaigns won, enemies vanquished, and nobles victorious, all from
the back of this valiant partner and warrior.

And now one of them, Eclipse, is my partner, my friend, my
horse.

This now stunning black mare first opened her eyes to the world
in 2003. On a cool spring morning, a gangly, long-legged, coal black
filly took her initial breath of life on our Crystal Peaks Youth Ranch
in central Oregon. I was the first human she came in contact with.
While I am careful about overemphasizing the philosophy of im-
printing, I was afforded the remarkable privilege of spending time
with her as she took her first steps and enjoyed her first meal. Forever
imprinted in my mind and on my heart is the mental picture of her
head in my lap as she snored away her first nap.

Eclipse was the last of five siblings born from an incredible mare
named C.B. (which stood for "City Blues"). Given to us as a gift,

C.B. was one of the first horses to come to the ranch. Thereafter, for eleven years C.B. was the alpha mare and herd boss to our little band of younger horses we called "the nursery." Sadly, a few years ago, I was forced to make the difficult decision to humanely end her life. At the mature age of twenty-two, she suffered severe arthritis that had chained her to days filled with pain and struggle. Her once-powerful and athletic frame had been compromised by a disease I could not cure or adequately manage.

Time and space have yet to heal the hole in my heart left by her passing. I deeply miss her.

The small arena that Eclipse and I train in is called a round pen. Simply described, it's a fifty-foot-diameter circular enclosure with eight-foot-high solid walls. Created for soft yet stable footing, the floor is a mixture of gravel and washed sand.

The general purposes of a round pen vary. While some folks may appreciate the safety or prefer the relatively small size of the round pen for exercising a horse, for me there is a deeper, more complete reason. It's common knowledge that horses are prey to other animals. With eyes on the sides of their head, horses, cattle, sheep, rabbits, and the like are built for seeing the world with an almost 270-degree perspective. With their complex optical systems, these creatures can see in front as well as behind themselves. Conversely, the predator, with eyes in front, sees the world with straight-ahead, tunnel vision.

You and I, because we have eyes in front, are considered predators by the equine. Therefore to a horse, we can be extremely intimidating and frightening. Horses, in addition, have a God-given desire for flight. They would rather run away than fight an approaching predator. Given these DNA-based differences, you can see how it can be potentially very difficult for a man, viewed as a predator, to foster a meaningful relationship with a horse, the prey.

The fragile relationship between horse and man is always precarious, and for eons mankind has struggled to coexist well with the equine. At one time horses were a basic food source for Neolithic man; they were hunter and prey. Over the centuries man has worked to dominate the noble equine, and the ancient methodology was archaic and brutal. But times have changed. It is with respect and deep gratitude that all horsemen can thank men like Buck Brannaman, Ray Hunt, Tom Dorrance, John Lyons, Klaus Ferdinand Hempfling, and others for providing us with the tools to better communicate with horses. These intuitive men have built a bridge, however tenuous, from human to equine.

While these great pioneers of natural horsemanship have been instrumental in creating the bridge, the use of it, in my humble opinion, is best experienced in the round pen. Created to provide a space for learning, the round pen can be a safe and secure training environment for both the horseman and the horse. While I am convinced of its usefulness for training our horses, I was completely unaware of the subtle yet life-changing lessons I would learn about myself and my Creator within the simple walls of this educational coliseum.

Standing quietly next to me in the walled circle, Eclipse boldly and confidently mirrors the strength, courage, and presence of her mother, C.B. Eclipse is quiet and attentive, her ears giving subtle clues as to what she's feeling and thinking. With the rush of the wind, her ears move. The call of a hawk flying over causes her to turn her head to listen. As I rub her muzzle and forehead, her eyes soften and her ears relax.

For thousands of years, men—through a lack of

understanding—compromised the fragile bond that once existed between horse and human. Yet here Eclipse stands, quietly in my care and presence. At anytime she could choose to walk away, to leave the safe sanctuary at my side. She chooses to stay.

EDUCATED IN THE ROUND PEN

There are countless potential teaching moments to savor within the confines of the round pen. One foundational understanding is that the best place—the safest, most secure space of quiet—is right at the trainer's side. It is imperative that Eclipse learn this very simple yet critical lesson. No matter what is going on around her, she must understand that safety and solace are at my side. If she chooses to not stay with me, her herd boss, she risks facing whatever is going on outside my care.

When Eclipse and I are in the round pen, it is my job to help her understand when it is best to move and when to stand quietly. Critical to the success of this basic lesson is for me to let her make the decision. With confinement aids, I could force her to stay with me, but that would teach her submission by fear and intimidation. Such was the case for hundreds of years.

While this horse domination methodology was effective in the short term, it proved to be destructive in creating a long-term, healthy relationship with the horse. Because at this stage of her training I choose to not use any man-made aids (such as halters, ropes, or reins), Eclipse has the choice to stay with me or not. That simple choice leads to trust, respect, and understanding. If she makes a different choice—the choice to leave my side, the choice to move without my leading—my response is simple: time to get back to work.

After she moved away from me, I—without emotion—would

honor her choice by asking her to move out, to get back to work. Or by sending her away I could, once again, give her the opportunity to choose to be with me or not.

At times she did choose to snort, kick up her heels, and run in circles around me. You could almost hear her saying, "So what do you think about that, boss?" Or maybe she said, "I am going to do it my own way! What are you going to do about it?"

"Well, that's okay, Eclipse. I am going to allow you to work, maybe even ask you to move out a bit more."

It's funny how all of that running in circles becomes hard work that gets her nowhere. Sooner or later, in a lathered-up, sweaty mess, she will stop, turn, and face me. And after a gentle lowering of my eyes, she is afforded the choice to quietly walk to my side.

Interesting. Here I was working to teach my equine partner a simple lesson of trust, and I found myself face to face with the realization that this lesson was for me. Like a hammer blow to the heart, I was reminded of the promises of Jesus:

- "I will never leave you or forsake you."
- "I will call you My own."
- "Seek first the kingdom of God."

The Lord was saying to me, "Troy, you run in circles all around Me. Every day you try to do it your way. You get all lathered up, sweaty, and exhausted in your day-to-day life, not realizing that life begins at My side. Not unlike you with Eclipse, I give you the unfettered ability to choose life at My side...or not!"

In the embrace of that simple lesson, the Lord of all gently reminded me, "Troy, My son, peace, joy, contentment, and safety can only be found at My side."

I was forced to ask myself, Just how many years have I chosen to leave the presence of Christ and do it all on my own? How many years have I wasted while my Creator, my Savior quietly waited for me?

Beyond Success

As men, so often we choose the life of a loner. We embrace an existence that resembles a man living on a deserted island. There we sit, day after day, with nothing but our newspaper, TV, a pizza, and the dog. We grumble at the kids, give our wife a peck on the cheek, and then escape to the solitary life. We run in a circle in our round pen of life, seeking to do what satisfies our often-selfish focus. All by our stubborn selves, we run and run around in circles, trying to find meaning and purpose.

Our career is one big cause of this isolation. How many times have you or I blamed our exhaustion, frustration, and exasperation on our job? A career is good; allowing it to control every part of our life is not. Don't misunderstand me here. In a world full of lazy slackers who would rather live on welfare and food stamps than by the sweat of the brow, working hard at one's job is a noble thing. My concern is that we get so caught up in the adrenaline fix success gives that we forget the most important and truly rewarding things in life.

Career success has many faces: the corner office, the next raise, the company car, the year-end bonus. All of these pursuits, while good in the right context, can force us to forget the peace and contentment found in the middle of life's round pen. We get ourselves so worked up in the pursuit of possessions, power, and prestige. Again, don't get me wrong. Success in one's chosen vocation is a good thing. My concern is that we often forsake the very *best things* in life for the pursuit of the seemingly *good things*.

Success, with all its rewards, seems so close we can almost touch it. But then, like a phantom in our dreams, it eludes us. We work so hard for something that, when found, rarely satisfies. Not unlike that greyhound chasing the rabbit, we forget everything and everyone around us as we circle time and again in life's round pen, seeking after what is right in front of our worn-out, reddened eyes.

John Rockefeller, one of the richest men who ever lived, was once asked, "Just how much money is enough?" His sad yet revealing response was, "Just one dollar more."

I wonder if Mr. Rockefeller ever knew true peace. In his lifelong pursuit of just one more dollar, I wonder if he ever stopped running in circles long enough to embrace existence for what it was meant to be. Or did he, not unlike my Eclipse, run blindly in circles around the One who wanted so deeply to have him at His side?

LISTENING TO GOD

Scripture vividly records the journey of a man who knew great success, only later to find himself hiding in a cave alone, deep in despair. After standing on a mountain and calling fire from heaven to consume the bad guys, the prophet Elijah tucked tail and ran in fear of Queen Jezebel. Scared for his life, Elijah ended up deep inside a cave on Mount Sinai, the mountain of God. Hmm, right smack-dab in the middle of God's round pen.

First Kings 19 tells how God met with our prophet-on-the-run. Elijah heard the Creator not in the fire, the windstorm, or the loud earthquakes of life. He heard the Lord quietly calling him in the whisper of the breeze. God was at the center of all the commotion and waiting patiently!

When was the last time you took a moment to simply stop and listen to creation? When was the last time you spent some time in the handbook, the Bible, over a cup of coffee and watched the sunrise? I am not talking about some men's book your buddy suggested you read. I am talking about the uncompromising, unchanging, ever-sharp, challenging Word of God. Yes…the Bible. I beg you, please don't waste your time reading this or any other book if it is replacing time spent in *the* Book.

No man, no movement, no "new thang" can ever replace the words written by Jesus Christ through the pen of the men He inspired. His Word is the center.

Time with Him, in His Word, early in the morning or sometime during the day, is the thing the enemy will fight the hardest to keep you from. Rest assured, friend, there will be every reason imaginable shoved in your face as to why you should not spend time in God's Word. Satan and his minions will work tirelessly to make sure you don't stop running around your pen long enough to stand quietly at the side of your Creator. Kick the ugly bum in the teeth and seek Jesus in the morning!

When was the last time you purposely forgot the tyranny of the urgent to stop and turn your face to Christ and walked to His side? Instead of trying to escape your troubles in the latest James Cameron movie, a hunting adventure, a car show, or an Internet site, how about spending some time at the side of Jesus?

Don't get me wrong; I am not some whacked-out dude who sits on a hill, eating granola, and singing, "Kum Bah Ya," all the time! I *love* car shows, steelhead fishing, and upland bird hunting. I hoot and holler at every Oregon Ducks football game I can take the time to see. I find great joy in riding my horse, hiking the Cascade Mountains, and working on my 1956 International pickup. However, I have learned from years of being an idiot that the best thing I can do for my life is to set my eyes on Jesus and walk to His side. It is there that I find true peace, wisdom, and strength.

In those uncomplicated moments in God's round pen, I find clarity and peace within the whispers of a timeless message from the Lord. Life exists in the presence of the King.

Gently the quiet breeze of an early fall morning in central Oregon begins to blow. Off in the distance I hear the familiar sounds of our small herd of horses shuffling about. Looking around the opening of the round pen, I see Lightfoot and Remnant playing tug of war with one of the Jolly Balls left in their paddock. Little Bear stretches as he gets up from an early morning nap. Jed and Mateo canter circles around Templeton and his mom.

The sun is making its way over the small butte behind the ranch. Off to the west the Three Sisters glow in the warm morning sun. It is perfect.

Eclipse, still at my side, softly nuzzles my shoulder. Her eyes never leave mine. In that incredible moment, time stands still. I recall an Arabian proverb I heard years ago:

> Horses—if God made anything more
> beautiful, He kept it for Himself.

In that simple moment, I am in awe of the depth of richness communicated between Eclipse and me. By her own choice, she stands at my side—peaceful, content, and at rest. I wonder, Does the Creator feel the same when we choose to set aside all the distractions of life, to stop running in circles, to step back from the demands of career, money, and the pursuit of success, when we choose to look into the eyes of pure love and joy and stand at His side? Does He look into our eyes and whisper, "I have never made anything more beautiful than you"?

With a subtle move of my hands, I ask Eclipse to gently move off. It is time, once again, to go to work. By her body language she questions me, unsure if I am certain it is time. With another gentle move of my hand, I assure her, yes, it is time to go to work, time to get into the lessons of the day. Her movement is fluid, powerful, and graceful. With such ease she responds to every motion of my hand. First at a walk, then trot, then canter, Eclipse once again tests the confines of the round pen. Her movement is controlled, at ease, confident.

Does she know? Does she understand? How could she ever realize that she is the living, breathing realization of a dream? She is a gift to me from the Giver of life...and dreams. All my life I had waited for her, and now she is here.

As Eclipse and I ended our time together in the round pen, I felt richer, fuller, and more complete. Jesus, the King of kings, had met me through the simple lesson I was trying to teach my equine partner. In my efforts to teach her, I had become the student. In all my years of running in circles, I had forgotten that wisdom, joy, peace, and rest are found while walking side by side with the King.

In a world of storms, in the round pens of life, all is well at the side of the Master.

14

The Rock

FOR MORE THAN A DECADE, Josh Thompson was the best.

In the world of men's biathlon, Josh repeatedly placed higher in World Cup standings than any American. To this day his achievements as a biathlete have yet to be eclipsed by any male or female produced by the United States. He is the greatest American biathlete ever.

If you are unfamiliar with the military-born sport of biathlon, it is a simple yet borderline psychotic form of competition. In brief terms, biathlon is the combined sport of rifle marksmanship and cross-country skiing. Carrying a rifle on your back, you cross-country ski until you feel like you are going to puke. Then you unsling your rifle, load it, and—while gasping for air and with a heart rate that's in the stratosphere—you stand and shoot with open sights at a saucer-sized target fifty meters away. And of course it's not a good idea to pass out in the process!

After blazing away at five targets, you release the clip, sling your rifle on your back, and head out for another pleasant three- to six-mile ski, after which you shoot again. This time, though, you are in the prone position, trying to hit a target the size of a fifty-cent piece at fifty meters.

Oh, and I forgot to mention that if you miss targets, you must ski penalty laps or, in the worst case, have extra minutes added to your time.

Sounds like a whole bunch of fun, doesn't it? I can tell you with utmost certainty, because I was stubborn enough to attempt it several times, that biathlon is the most difficult sport I have ever tried! It was an ugly picture: I lumbered down the trail, all six foot three, 230 pounds of me, sounding like some sick freight train. Guys like Josh, lithe, fit, and graceful, cruised by with poetic motion as this dingrod fool tried to do something God *never* created him for. For goodness sake, I was designed as a linebacker, not a cross-country skier!

I met Josh in West Yellowstone in 1989. He was skiing in the same mountain training camp as my wife, Kim. Oh, I forgot to mention, she was one of those crazy biathletes too. For a short time she competed with the best female athletes in the United States, but that is a whole different story.

When I first crossed paths with Josh, he was a twenty-something, self-confident, stringy blond-haired king of the course. Everyone wanted to be his friend. He walked the streets of that small mountain town with a posse ten layers deep. He and Kim had struck up a wonderful friendship. She spoke often in her letters home how Josh had taken her and others snowmobiling, hiking, even flying. Yes, with all his world-class talent in alpine sports, the guy was also a flight instructor. In fact, flying was his "real" job. When he wasn't traveling the world, competing with the planet's finest, he was home, giving flight lessons in the high back country of Colorado.

FLYING HIGH

One fall back in the 1990s, Kim and I went to Gunnison, Colorado, to spend a few days with Josh, his wife, Carolyn, and their two boys,

Cole and Risto. Because Josh has such a deep passion for flying, I felt it prudent—okay, maybe a bit selfish—to take some time and get up in the air. It had been a lifelong dream of mine to fly, and after years of waiting, I was now accumulating hours for a private pilot's license. So Josh's suggestion that we take a few afternoons and go flying was met with a resounding "You bet!" from me! What guy in his right mind would ever pass up the chance to fly a plane in the Colorado Rockies? *Not me!*

For three memorable sunny afternoons we flew together—sailing over icy, trout-filled rivers, deep canyons, and soaring mountaintops. The everyday cares of life faded into distant memories as we navigated our little magic carpet over the imposing landscape. The consummate instructor, Josh gave me learning experiences I will never forget.

The Gunnison-Crested Butte Regional Airport is in a shallow, high-desert bowl surrounded by foothills and then the higher peaks of the Colorado Rockies. At 7,700 feet above sea level, the Gunnison area is a perfect place to hone one's mountain flying skills. During my flying time with Josh, I practiced takeoffs, landings, and touch and go's. With his help I also executed simple and complex flying maneuvers, including a few stalls and stomach-churning spins. I was in heaven.

On our third and final flight, we went far north of the airport, the populated areas of Gunnison, and the small town of Baldwin. We pushed our little rented Cessna 172 hard as we climbed higher and higher into the backwoods of the Colorado wilderness.

I was mesmerized by the unimaginable beauty of the earth passing beneath us. We cruised over desert hues of brown, sage, and gold. From there we traveled higher into the hidden mountain sanctuaries of green old-growth forests, vertical granite rock faces, and the deep blue of ancient high-mountain lakes. The scenery was staggering.

I had dreamed of doing this since I was a kid. Now, as we flew, I often found myself on the verge of tears, thanking God for His kindness in allowing one of my lifelong dreams to come true. Our Father in heaven longs to give us the desires of our heart, but He definitely does this on His terms and with His timing. He is God; I am not.

AN UNFORGETTABLE LESSON

Josh never knew that those times of soaring among the clouds were some of the most impressionable days of my life. For a man who had long dreamed of escaping the gravitational bonds of earth, to soar where the eagle and the hawk fly, and to skirt the boundaries of the rain clouds, these memories are forever etched in my mind and heart.

And there's also the memory of one particular lesson learned near the rock walls of a high mountain gorge...

Josh had filed a flight plan that, unknown to me, took us into the heart of the Rockies, west of Mount Emmons and south of Peeler Peak. This indescribable part of Colorado is only a few miles east of Crested Butte and a short flight from Aspen. Our destination was a large alpine canyon that Josh for years had used as a perfect place to teach students some of the finer lessons of technical mountain flying.

As we eased the 172 into the entrance to the canyon, Josh, with typical Thompson dry humor, gave me my instructions for this final flight lesson: "Okay, Mr. Top Gun," I heard him say in my David Clark headset, "here is the scenario. You have flown into a deep mountain canyon with the weather closing in behind you. You must cross over a mountain pass to safety. Your dilemma is that you don't have the power to do so with safe altitude. Your aircraft is theoretically at its maximum operational ceiling. The only way out is to find warm afternoon updrafts. When you find them, they will give you the lift needed to fly over the pass. You are only a VFR pilot, so flying back through the clouds is not an option. Recall your weather training, and find the thermals. It is early afternoon, so they are there."

In the afternoons of late summer and early fall days, high-mountain thermals are fairly predictable. As the sun starts its lazy disappearance in the latter part of the day, the southern- and western-facing slopes warm up. The sun creates an upwelling of temperate wind that arrives, like clockwork, on the exposed slopes. A capable pilot can find these gentle breezes and use them to safely assist an aircraft up and over dangerous coulee walls.

After a few moments of orientation, weather observation, and trim, fuel, and speed checks, I cleared the airspace around us and slowly began to move the plane to an exposed area of the canyon that I thought would give us the thermals we needed. Facing southwest and bright with the late-day sun, it seemed the perfect spot to find them. As we neared the canyon wall, I gently banked the plane left toward the sun. Flying with our belly and right wing, what seemed like a few hundred feet from the wall, I could feel no lift. At ten thousand feet above mean sea level, the oxygen-starved Cessna was barely able to maintain our current altitude, let alone climb higher.

As we leveled out at the end of our mountain arena, I banked hard left to send us down toward our original entrance. The first circle around the canyon walls had been a bust. We had not gained any altitude at all.

Josh jokingly quipped, "Well, it's a good thing we weren't in trouble, because otherwise we'd probably be dead." What a comedian. "Let's make things a bit more realistic. What do you think?" he said with his trademark cunning grin. "Let's take another trip around the block, but this time with a little less power." With that, he reached down and dropped the rpm's of our already underpowered aircraft.

The burr in my saddle just got bigger. Keep in mind that Josh had several thousand hours of flying Cessna 172s. Our little puddle-jumper was his office. He knew every inch, every flight characteristic, every weakness and strength of our airborne machine.

Making a hard left turn, I set us up for another pass. This time, with less power to work with, stalling the aircraft became one more item on a long list of flight management issues. It would be easy to ask the struggling aircraft for more altitude, only to force a potentially fatal stall. With Josh's hands close by the yoke, I eased the 172 even closer to the ominous granite walls. With eyes on altitude, speed, rpm's, and the deadly canyon face, I was confident we were close enough this time. The right wingtip seemed only a few feet away from the sheer face passing by at 100 mph. Because forbidden terrain heightens the senses, what seemed like a few feet was actually more.

"Come on, baby," I heard myself mutter into the mic.

"Closer, Troy. You gotta get closer," Josh gently but firmly demanded. "You gotta get close to the rock."

"I am close," I protested.

"No, you're not, my friend. Check your altimeter." Our altitude had not changed. In fact, because he'd cut back on the power, we were losing precious distance from the forest floor. And still no thermals. Banking the plane left again, we circled for one more try.

"You have to make this one work, Troy," Josh implored. "If this were a life-or-death situation, you wouldn't have a choice. You must find the updraft out of this canyon."

Sweat dripped from my face. My neck and back muscles, once loose and relaxed, were tight with tension. My hold on the yoke had turned from the required gentle touch to a death grip.

"Ease up, big boy. This is supposed to be fun!" Josh quipped.

"Fun? Are you crazy? You've got me flying up here, no power, high altitude…trying to hit the side of a mountain. You bonehead, I thought we were supposed to stay *away* from Mother Earth!"

With a characteristic Thompson chuckle, Josh said, "Take a deep breath. This is fun. And no worries! I am certainly not going to let you hit the side of the mountain. Okay, Junior Birdman, one more try. This time, I know you can get us up and over."

Once more we circled from the right to the left, setting up for one more pass. As I turned the aircraft into the northwest heading, the sun was beginning its drop into evening, and the late afternoon glow was brilliant on the granite face. With backpressure applied, I made a slight dip of the yoke to the left. I touched a little left rudder in and eased the plane parallel to the wall to maintain an easy escape left. With all the body language I could muster, I almost willed the Cessna to the warm side of the mountain.

"Closer…just a little closer," Josh whispered into my headset.

"I can't, Josh!"

"Yes, you can! You must, Troy. If we are ever going to make this work, you gotta get close to the rock. Ease the yoke a bit more right, ease up a bit on the rudder, and just let her slide closer."

As the canyon wall closed in, I relaxed and edged the plane one final push toward the rock face. With the wingtip seemingly inches away from the ancient gray stone, the granite flying by in a blur, Josh quietly said, "There it is…there you go…you made it."

Then it happened. Like a gentle breath rising from the canyon floor, at first with no sensation of rising, the updraft first cushioned and then lifted us smoothly above the ridge. Easing back into my seat, relaxing the yoke, I saw the altimeter spin clockwise. We were ascending. Without my increasing power or pulling back on the yoke, the plane was rising! As if lifted by the mighty hand of God, our trip around the canyon ended as we breached the top of the granite walls and soared above the treetops.

Reaching down, I added power as we made a gentle turn left toward home. In my headset I could hear a chuckle. "What are you grinning at, you skinny flyboy?" I asked Josh, seeing the grin on his face.

"Oh, just laughing at you. You look like you just won the lottery or something."

After a few seconds, I took a deep breath and smiled back. "Thank you, Josh. Thanks to you, I just did."

With the sun setting at our right and the intense green of the high-mountain forest floor fading to the warm hues of the desert, we pointed our small dream maker home. The Gunnison airport appeared, and I will never forget, as I turned us onto the final approach, the feeling I had deep inside me. With flaps at ten…twenty…then thirty degrees, engine rpm's at 1500, carb heat on, we touched down and rolled to a stop just as the sun made its final hurrah.

With a smile and a firm handshake, Josh congratulated me on a nice flight. "Well done, friend. I would fly with you any day."

To this day I am so thankful that dark sunglasses hid the tears of an old cowboy, an average Joe who for one afternoon lived his dream of being a mountain pilot.

Stay Close to the Rock

Flying in Colorado that warm fall day, I learned that in order for us to find the updraft that would lift Josh and me out of trouble, I needed to get closer to the rock. I needed to put us both in what seemed to be a dangerous situation for us to be able to reach safety.

A deeper relationship with Christ is not unlike that flight in the canyon.

As men, our first step into embracing and finding fulfillment in the life of an average Joe is to get close to the Rock, the rock that is Jesus Christ. King David said, "The LORD is my rock, my fortress, and my savior; my God is my rock, in whom I find protection" (Psalm 18:2).

Life is hard. I get that. It seems as though around every corner there waits one more unexpected bill, one more job challenge, one more argument with our spouse. And, candidly, that's the small stuff. What about our very life? What about our eternal destination? Jesus said, "I am the way, the truth, and the life. No one can come to the Father except through me" (John 14:6).

Did you hear that, average Joe? There is no other way to find true peace, abiding joy, and deep contentment than in the embrace of your Creator. There is no salvation outside the Savior, Jesus Christ. If you understand nothing else within the pages of this book, understand this: Jesus Christ is the Rock of our salvation. He *is* the one and *only* son of God. He *is* the only way to eternal life. Life begins at the Rock, at the Cross.

If we are ever going to find the gentle, warm breeze that will lift us out and above the daily struggles of this world into the place God is calling us—into strength as men of God—we have to find Jesus Christ, our Rock. He is the cornerstone of our salvation. He is the granite face that evil crashes against. He is the immovable One.

While His Word certainly speaks of mercy, joy, and peace—a life in service to Him—flying close to the Rock can be dodgy, challenging, and even dangerous. The Word of God is quite clear in that, by following Christ, we may lose friends, comfort, family, even our life. However, a life sold out for Jesus is the very best life we can live.

We were created by God, to be with God. You are not some product of evolution that by chance came from some primordial pool of goo some fifty billion years ago. You are God's very best creation. He delights in you. Read Psalm 139 if you really want to see how much God loves you!

We must get close to Him. Once we choose to embrace the calling God has for us, we can do *nothing* outside the strength and power of Jesus Christ. The apostle Paul wrote a timeless verse in his passionate letter of joy to the Philippians: "For I can do everything with the help of Christ who gives me the strength I need" (4:13).

If your life seems boring, uneventful, without purpose, I challenge you to take a chance. Fly that little puddle-jumper you call "existence" a little closer to the Rock that is Jesus Christ.

AVERAGE JOE STUDY GUIDE

UNDERSTANDING YOUR STUDY GUIDE

This study guide is designed to be used *after* the designated chapters assigned to each session have been read. Whether you are studying *Average Joe* as an individual or in a group, the goal is to dive deeper, wrestle harder, and sense God's presence and affirmation as you process and pray about what you are learning.

The study guide has eight sessions. However, if your group wants to move more slowly, just adjust the reading assignments and questions accordingly.

Read the Chapters
Each session (except sessions 1 and 6) will cover two chapters of *Average Joe*. As you read the chapters, make notes or highlight passages in the book that speak to, challenge, or apply to you *personally*. In your reading and reflection, ask the Lord to reveal insights so that when you come to the study guide section, you will be equipped to benefit the most from the questions.

Introduction and General Feedback
After you have welcomed the group and asked about answers to prayer from prior sessions, spend some time in prayer together. Next, have someone read the brief introduction aloud to remind everyone

of the focus of the discussion. The leader should then invite the group to share any questions, concerns, "aha" insights, or comments arising out of their personal time with the material.

A Man and His Story

Since *Average Joe* includes a number of compelling stories, it is natural and wise to make sure the men in the group have an opportunity to share the story of their own journey. It's suggested that during each session one man be given the floor and up to ten minutes to provide some background about his life. Some men will want to speak far less; others will want to have more time. As the facilitator of the group, remind each man before he begins to be honest, to go beyond surface details, to share the good and the bad, to include his spiritual testimony, and to try to stay within the ten-minute limit. As the leader, you may need to encourage some men to offer more detail by asking questions along the way. You also may need to encourage others to be more concise in the interest of time. Perhaps you, as the leader, should tell your story first to model the process. Remember, the purpose of this group is to go deep. No one has the time for just another breakfast with the boys.

Go Through the Questions

The questions are designed to focus on how each person related to the main topics of the chapters. Remember, the questions are there to serve the group and encourage discussion, not to elicit a particular answer. With that in mind, *don't race through the questions*. Take your time, and allow the Holy Spirit to work. Also, it is not necessary to go around the circle or table and have everyone answer before you move on to the next question. The best interaction is going to occur when men feel free to speak their hearts.

The group discussion is actually an opportunity to allow God's Spirit to minister uniquely through one believer to another in very specific ways. Relax and trust God to take the discussion where He wants it to go. Remember, if God isn't in this, you are probably wasting your time. If you don't get through all the questions in a session, no worries.

The Truth

Each session will have a theme verse that connects to the content. Groups should read the verse out loud, and if someone in the group has a different Bible translation, ask him to read it aloud so the group can get a bigger picture of the meaning of the passage. You may want to encourage the men to memorize these verses.

Close Each Session in Prayer

Praying together is the most powerful way to make what you are learning effective, meaningful, authentic, and relevant. Do not leave too little time for prayer! Be sure the men have the opportunity to share their requests. Expect God to hear and respond to your prayers.

Session 1
Who Is Average Joe?

Note: Please read chapter 1 of *Average Joe* prior to session 1.

Introduction

The theme of this book is that living an "average," "ordinary," or "normal" life should not cause any of us to feel that we have missed God's plan or that somehow our lives have no purpose or might even be called a failure. In fact, by living a steady, faithful, God-honoring life of integrity and service, a man accomplishes great things for the kingdom. Our Lord seems to have a particular fondness for people that the rest of the world tends to overlook. Consider what the apostle Paul wrote:

> Remember, dear brothers and sisters, that few of you were wise in the world's eyes, or powerful, or wealthy when God called you. Instead, God deliberately chose things the world considers foolish in order to shame those who think they are wise. And he chose those who are powerless to shame those who are powerful. God chose things despised by the world, things counted as nothing at all, and used them to bring to nothing what the world considers important, so that no one can ever boast in the presence of God. (1 Corinthians 1:26–29)

In the sessions of this study, we will look at examples of men from the Bible and men from today as we explore just what it means to be an average Joe.

A Man's Story

It's up to the members of your group to decide, but since so much of the message of the book *Average Joe* is communicated through stories told by Troy Meeder about his life and the lives of other men, we encourage each man in your group to share his story. It's suggested that about ten minutes of each session be given to one man to give the broad outline of his story—where he was born, his family, his growing-up experiences, his education and work, his faith, and his life today. It's important to not just give the surface details but to also share some of the behind-the-scenes details about traumas, joys, disappointments, dreams, and so on. Be sure, too, to encourage each man to include information on his personal spiritual journey with the Lord.

Questions

1. After reading chapter 1 in the book, describe an average Joe in your own words.

2. What are the qualities of a man who is an average Joe?

3. Why might it be wrong to describe an average Joe as unmotivated, incompetent, inconsequential, lazy, mediocre, and so on?

Troy shares this observation:

> What happened for most of us is *reality*. Instead of finding fame and fortune, normalcy and "never enough" found us.

4. Life does serve up many challenges and disappointments. Have you ever asked yourself, "What happened to my life?" What prompted that question?

5. What has been your general response to the fact that your life has, in certain ways, been different from what you once imagined?

In *Average Joe* we read this:

> God seems to have a special fondness for average Joes. Before
> they accomplished extraordinary deeds, normal guys like
> Gideon, David, Peter, and Paul went about their farming,
> sheep herding, fishing, and tent making. Even Jesus, our
> Redeemer, Healer, and coming King, started out using a
> hammer and saw in a carpenter's shop.

6. How do you respond to the idea that these "famous" men of
   the Bible were actually fairly ordinary until God set them
   apart for His service?

7. Is it a man's *abilities* or his *willingness* that qualifies him to
   serve God effectively? Explain your answer.

The TRUTH

The LORD doesn't make decisions the way you do! People
judge by outward appearance, but the LORD looks at a
person's thoughts and intentions. (1 Samuel 16:7)

Prayer
Share your needs and requests, and close in prayer. This is critical.
Spending time together with the Father is essential to building community and growing in faith.

To prepare for the next study and discussion,
read chapters 2 and 3 in *Average Joe*.

Session 2
Dreams and Disappointments

Note: Please read chapters 2 and 3
of *Average Joe* prior to session 2.

Introduction

Dreams are powerful and can provide a man with the focus and fuel to achieve amazing things. The dilemma is that not all our dreams come true—or they haven't come true on our time schedule. As men, how do we deal with unrealized dreams?

A Man's Story

Whose turn is it this time? Based on the instructions given under this heading in the introduction and session 1, please ask another man in the group to share his story. Give him about ten minutes to share.

Questions

1. What dreams for your future did you have as a boy?

2. When you were a boy and later a young man, what did you think you would have to do to prove you had become a man?

Troy writes the following:

It is intriguing to watch the intense, extreme, never-compromising focus the greyhound has as it chases its target. As if its life depends on catching the fleeting quarry, the greyhound runs with complete abandonment.

3. What are some things you have chased in your life?

4. Troy recounts the story of Peter, who in the space of a few hours went from being a "somebody"—one of Jesus's chosen confidants—to being a cowardly betrayer. Have you had situations like this in life when failure or disappointment suddenly replaced success and satisfaction? Share some stories.

5. Troy shares that becoming a youth pastor made him feel like he was "the man"—solidly in the center of God's will and plans. Have you ever had a similar experience in your life?

6. Troy tells of almost being swallowed up—literally—in a huge hole. What holes, figuratively speaking, have you fallen into in your life? How did you get out? What did you learn?

7. Why is adversity such an effective teacher?

The TRUTH

And we know that God causes everything to work together for the good of those who love God and are called according to his purpose for them. (Romans 8:28)

Prayer

Share requests and pray for one another.

To prepare for the next study and discussion,
read chapters 4 and 5 in *Average Joe.*

Session 3
Solid and Steady

Note: Please read chapters 4 and 5
of *Average Joe* prior to session 3.

Introduction

In addition to their unwavering commitment to follow and obey God, average Joes always seem to display two key qualities: integrity and steadiness. In the chapters assigned for this session, Troy shares the stories of two ordinary men—a gardener and a grandfather—who lived out these exemplary qualities. What can we learn from their lives?

A Man's Story

Give the floor to another man in your group to tell his story.

Questions

1. What did you find interesting and helpful in the stories about Jim the gardener and Ray, Troy's grandfather?

Troy explains that he learned certain standards for his life from Jim the gardener:

- Let your yes be yes and your no be no.
- Your handshake is your bond.
- The body of Christ is a tapestry of living creatures all joined together by the blood thread of Jesus.
- Everyone needs a little manure in his or her life sometimes.

2. Which of these standards do you find most meaningful?

3. Are there other standards you would add to the list? What are they?

4. Inevitably, storms or difficult challenges and trials arise in life. When you are going through a storm, what would you say acts as your compass? What keeps you from getting off course?

5. Have you had situations where, without a solid moral compass, you would have been in big trouble? Talk about one of those situations.

Troy has this to say about how men lose their way in life:

> As men, we so often compromise. We rationalize in our
> mind that "it's only a little sin." No one will ever know. That
> voice whispers in our ear:
>
> - "Come on, buddy. Everyone does it. So what if you
>   cheat a little on your tax return?"
> - "It really is no big deal that you take your secretary to
>   an early dinner...to that really intimate little bistro on
>   the coast. So what if you have a few drinks, tell an
>   off-color joke or two, and marvel at the sunset. I mean,
>   come on, dude, she really gets you. Your wife doesn't."
> - "Who cares if you surf the Web and hang out for a
>   bit on those sites that you know you shouldn't? You
>   deserve a little break!"
>
> Or do you?
>
> Here's what the Bible has to say about this: "But now you
> must be holy in everything you do, just as God—who chose
> you to be his children—is holy.... And remember that the
> heavenly Father to whom you pray has no favorites when he
> judges. He will judge or reward you according to what you
> do. So you must live in reverent fear of him during your time
> as foreigners here on earth" (1 Peter 1:15, 17).

6. Whose voice is it that seeks to lure you into a life of
   compromise?

7. What are some effective ways to fight off temptation? These
   verses have some clues:

Be careful! Watch out for attacks from the Devil, your great enemy. He prowls around like a roaring lion, looking for some victim to devour. Take a firm stand against him, and be strong in your faith. Remember that your Christian brothers and sisters all over the world are going through the same kind of suffering you are. (1 Peter 5:8–9)

Don't be fooled by those who say such things, for "bad company corrupts good character." (1 Corinthians 15:33)

And let us not neglect our meeting together, as some people do, but encourage and warn each other, especially now that the day of his coming back again is drawing near. (Hebrews 10:25)

A final word: Be strong with the Lord's mighty power. Put on all of God's armor so that you will be able to stand firm against all strategies and tricks of the Devil. (Ephesians 6:10–11)

The TRUTH

In the same way, let your good deeds shine out for all to see, so that everyone will praise your heavenly Father. (Matthew 5:16)

Prayer

Share requests and pray for one another.

To prepare for the next study and discussion,
read chapters 6 and 7 in *Average Joe*.

Session 4
Faithfulness and Honor

> Note: Please read chapters 6 and 7
> of *Average Joe* prior to session 4.

Introduction

It doesn't matter whether a particular average Joe is called upon to save a fellow soldier's life, rope a steer, fertilize the lawn, or help with a child's science project. A good man faithfully shows up and does what is right and what is required of him. That is the essence of honor.

A Man's Story

Whose turn is it this session? Enjoy hearing the story of another one of your brothers.

Questions

Troy writes this about average Joes:

> Without fanfare, they roll up their sleeves and get to the task at hand, no matter what it is. Finn and his comrades were getting ready to fight a war. You may just be dealing with a broken washing machine, a crabby boss, or a prideful teenager. It doesn't matter. Each of us has a job to do, no matter what it may be.

1. What responsibilities in your life do you as a man find relatively easy? What are the hard ones?

2. What strategies have helped you become more responsible about doing things that are hard for you?

In *Average Joe* we read this:

> In the books of Proverbs and Ecclesiastes, books rich in simple cowboy wisdom, Solomon speaks over and over of the futility of too many words, calling the man who talks too much a fool. The wise old king reminds us that fools talk a lot; the wise listen.

3. What can be the result of speaking the wrong words at the wrong time? Or, equally as important, what can be the result of speaking the right words at the right time?

Troy shares this insight:

> There are times in life when adhering to our principles can make existence difficult. We sometimes find ourselves at the wrong end of a joke. Or maybe we lose a business deal or a so-called friend. In an extreme situation, sticking to a principle might cost us our lives.

4. Take turns sharing a life experience when sticking to principles cost you something.

5. How did you find the strength to stand strong?

6. If there was a time when you failed to stand strong, what caused you to violate your principles?

In *Average Joe* we are asked to consider:

Jesus said, "You can enter God's Kingdom only through the narrow gate. The highway to hell is broad, and its gate is wide for the many who choose the easy way. But the gateway to life is small, and the road is narrow, and only a few ever find it'" (Matthew 7:13–14).

Too few men determine within themselves to live a life marked by purpose, wisdom, gentle strength, and unwavering faithfulness. These are the guys traveling on the high road. It saddens me, too, that I often have turned onto the highway of societal correctness, selfish sin, pride, and compromise when I should have driven hard on the two-lane road of certainty, of moral determination.

7. What do you think Jesus meant by the "narrow gate"? What do you think He meant by "highway"?

8. In what areas of your life do you want to move from the highway to the narrow gate?

The TRUTH

Let your "Yes" be yes, and your "No," no, or you will be condemned. (James 5:12, NIV)

Prayer

Share requests and pray for one another.

> To prepare for the next study and discussion,
> read chapters 8 and 9 in *Average Joe*.

Session 5
A Father and a Brother

> Note: Please read chapters 8 and 9
> of *Average Joe* prior to session 5.

Introduction

It may be something of a cliché, but it also happens to be true: *men need other men.* Perhaps one of the great spiritual tragedies of our generation is that spiritually mature men have not mentored younger, less mature men. This certainly was not the model presented by Jesus as He worked with His men. Jesus poured Himself into those often dull and stubborn disciples—the same guys who later went out and changed the world on His behalf.

But as important as it is to have a mentor in your life, it's just as critical to have a friend—a buddy—that you can hang with, laugh with, just be with.

We need them both: a mentor who's a father and a friend who's a brother.

A Man's Story

Listen carefully to another man's story. Sharing together in the journey of life brings courage and encouragement to stand strong.

Questions

1. Have you ever had an average Joe in your life who was a source of advice and wisdom to you? Explain what this man's wisdom meant to you.

Consider these words from *Average Joe:*

Mentors—men of wisdom and passion who are usually older—are all around us. We find them working part time at Home Depot or looking at some tackle at the local fly shop. They are elders in our churches, Boy Scout leaders, and volunteers at local charities. Most of them don't understand Blu-ray players, iPods, or Facebook. I guess they would rather talk with you face to face than through some "confounded computer."

2. If you were seeking a mentor, what qualities would you look for in that man?

Troy writes this:

The time-proven foundation of experiencing life together, either as the teacher or the student, is one that every man should be a part of. And, yes, even average Joes, men without all the supposed "right stuff," can be instrumental in the leadership of others. In fact, the very best mentors are those who would be considered average Joes.

3. Why might the best mentors be average Joes?

4. Why might it be a good idea for a Christian man to be both mentored himself as well as to mentor another man?

5. Do you feel qualified to be a mentor? Why or why not?

As important as mentoring is, friendship is also a key component of a man's life:

> As boys, we were able to create and enjoy lasting friendships. We found it easy to shoulder up with other guys down the road. Our days were filled with building forts, hiking in the hills behind our homes, riding bikes, surfing, whatever. We explored what was available in our neighborhood. We had good times and bad. Sometimes we fought; sometimes we cried. We shared our deepest thoughts, biggest dreams, and supported one another when we failed. We shared a lot of things, but most of all, we just lived. We were friends.
>
> I struggle sometimes with what has happened as we have grown up.
>
> Long gone are those days of simplicity. Erased from our memories are the times when we just enjoyed the company of a friend. Why? Why is it so hard to experience life with other guys as we once did?

6. Do you agree or disagree with Troy? Was it easier for you to make and enjoy friends when you were a boy?

Troy shares this observation in *Average Joe:*

I think we don't have real friends because we don't *try* to have real friends. Yep, that simple.

7. Do you agree or disagree with this quote? Give reasons for your answer.

Troy adds this:

All through the Bible, men are shown teaming up to accomplish the impossible for God: Moses and Aaron; David and Jonathan; Peter and John; Paul and Timothy; the three leaders of David's indomitable thirty mighty men—Jashobeam, Eleazar, and Abishai. And of course Jesus and His Twelve. We are *better* when we work together. We are at our *best* when we work together in the service of the One who has given us life, Jesus Christ. He is the common ground, the mortar that is foundational in building relationships that go the distance.

8. Why do you think we men are "at our *best* when we work together in the service of…Jesus Christ"?

The TRUTH

As iron sharpens iron, a friend sharpens a friend. (Proverbs 27:17)

Prayer

Share requests and pray for one another.

To prepare for the next study and discussion,
read chapter 10 in *Average Joe*.

Session 6
A Man and His Home

Note: Please read chapter 10
of *Average Joe* prior to session 6.

Introduction

Marriage is the most important human relationship most of us will ever embrace. We long for an intimacy with our spouse that surpasses anything we will experience with any other person. So why is marriage such a struggle at times? In this session we will unpack some truth about marriage as well as discuss the unique role every average Joe must assume as the leader of those who can find peace and protection under his covering.

A Man's Story

Enjoy another unique opportunity to learn from the life of another man in the group. Who's up today?

Questions

In chapter 10 of *Average Joe,* Troy describes a dark time in his marriage. And he writes of an issue many men face: pornography.

> My friend, the lure of what can be seen on the computer screen is an infection leading unto death. Trust me—it will rot your core. I have seen it happen time and time again to men. When

they walk that well-traveled superhighway of lust, their honor, self-respect, integrity, and resolve are all exchanged for some putrid excuse of manhood. Sadly, this depraved expressway to hell seldom includes just visual stimulation. Often what a man sees turns into what he does. He begins to compromise in every area of his life. Sinning becomes easier. All the while the covenant relationship between himself and the wife God gave him crumbles right in front of his eyes.

1. Pornography, especially on the Internet, is a big problem for men, even many Christian men. Why is porn such a lure?

2. Do you agree that porn often leads to compromising in every area of life? Explain your answer.

Troy shares this experience:

What a patient God we serve. For years, while I had run away from His side, He had been waiting for me. In a breath, He was there. I cried out; He answered. What is it about our God that He would lower Himself to meet with a broken, battered, selfish, prideful man...in the cab of an old Dodge pickup? That cold, snowy day in November, the King of kings put His arms around what was left of me...and the healing began.

I couldn't get home fast enough.

3. Why is it never too late to seek healing for problems in a marriage?

Consider this paragraph from *Average Joe:*

> Within the context of marriage, no failure in a relationship
> is one-sided. It always takes two. However, I strongly
> believe that the health of a marriage is directly related to
> the spiritual health and leadership of the husband, the
> "pastor" of the home. When things go south, more often
> than not, it is because we husbands have failed to embrace
> our role in the manner God intended.... We are to take on
> the mantle of authority over and responsibility for our
> family.

4. Do you agree or disagree that the "health of a marriage is
   directly related to the spiritual health and leadership of the
   husband"? Why do you feel this way?

5. What actions do you need to take to improve your relationship with your wife?

Now read this charge from *Average Joe:*

> As men we were created to be the covering for our families—
> the ones who shelter all those under our care from the storms
> of life. But that's the easy part. It's leading our loved ones to
> the foot of the cross that makes us men. Get your family to
> church. Better yet, be the pastor of your own home. Here is a
> novel one: *pray* with your family. Not just the casual "Hey,
> God, thanks for the grub!" I mean, do business with Jesus
> *with* your family.

6. What does it mean for a man to be the "covering" for his family?

7. In what practical ways can a man lead his "loved ones to the foot of the cross"?

We men cannot expect our wives or children to be more spiritually mature than we are. Troy makes these comments:

> Are you studying and meditating on God's Word every day? Yes, friend, *every* day! Do your kids, when they rise, see their father spending time with the Father? Or is the *New York Times,* the local news rag, or some ESPN talk show more important? Why should we fill our minds with worthless drivel instead of the priceless, powerful, life-changing Word of God?...
> The truth is, friend, *all* of us will one day stand before our Creator and be held accountable for how we have lived our lives. Our wives won't be there with us. Our children either. Nor friends, family, relatives. We will be alone.

8. Why do most of us find it difficult to maintain a consistent quality time of personal devotions—Bible study, prayer, and quiet reflection?

9. What practical things could you do to improve your walk with God?

The TRUTH

And you husbands must love your wives with the same love Christ showed the church. He gave up his life for her to make her holy and clean, washed by baptism and God's word. (Ephesians 5:25–26)

Prayer

Share requests and pray for one another.

To prepare for the next study and discussion, read chapters 11 and 12 in *Average Joe*.

Session 7
Beyond Fear

Note: Please read chapters 11 and 12 of *Average Joe* prior to session 7.

Introduction

In this session we discuss two important issues in every man's life: first, the need to face and conquer unexpected crises and the fear that accompanies them, and second, the challenge of looking beyond our own needs—even beyond the needs of those close to us—and responding to the needs of our broader community and even the world.

A Man's Story

Give another man in your group the opportunity to share his story.

Questions

Maybe these words from *Average Joe* describe you:

> Have you been there? Life was just truckin' along and—
> crack!—out of the blue, you got hit by a lightning bolt
> that caused you to run screaming to your momma.
> Maybe it was a tax audit, a bad medical report, a child
> caught with drugs, a companywide layoff, or—who knows?
> We just know that we panicked. We responded like little
> children and ran for cover into alcohol, work, an affair, or
> whatever.

1. Take turns sharing about a crisis that came out of the blue
   and rocked your world.

2. How did you respond to your crisis situation? What emotions did you have?

3. What is bad about fear? What is good about fear?

Now consider these words by Troy:

> It is easy, in the face of certain struggles, maybe even death, to
> panic. The hurricanes of life will rage. Crises will come. The
> true test of the man, the average Joe, is his response within the
> storm. Will you, will I, cower before the oncoming giant, or
> will we stand in the strength of Jesus Christ? Will you and I
> trust in the One who has already won the battle?

4. Do you find it difficult to trust Christ with your fears? Why or why not?

5. How can we as men help one another during times of fear and personal crisis?

6. In *Average Joe* the author tells of a missions trip to Sri Lanka. What do you think are the benefits of engaging in some type of missions activity, whether in your own community or elsewhere in the world?

In *Average Joe,* Troy writes:

We are men. We are the gatekeepers to our homes. We do what we do as fathers, sons, employees, employers— whether professional or blue collar. We fuss and muss about, worrying about the smallest things. We let things like bills, broken pipes, expected promotions, and politics consume our lives.

Yet, in all that we do and worry about, the single most important life calling is the handshake we have with God the Father when we look into His eyes and say, "Yes, yes, my King. I will take Your Son home with me. I will embrace Him as Lord of my life. I will embrace Him as the King of who I am. I will be the gatekeeper who opens the door for Him to come in and be in *my home,* with *my family.*

He will be *my Lord.*"

7. What does the term "the lordship of Christ" mean to you?

8. In what areas of your life do you want to see Christ's lordship expand?

The TRUTH

> For you did not receive a spirit that makes you a slave again to fear, but you received the Spirit of sonship. And by him we cry, "Abba, Father." (Romans 8:15, NIV)

Prayer

Share requests and pray for one another.

To prepare for the next study and discussion, read chapters 13 and 14 in *Average Joe*.

Session 8
Follow the King

Note: Please read chapters 13 and 14 of *Average Joe* prior to session 8.

Introduction

In the final chapters, the discussion moves to embracing the never-ending process of becoming more like Christ. Are we willing to allow God to use every means at His disposal to mold us into the image of His Son and become totally dependent on Him?

A Man's Story

This is the last opportunity for any men in the group to share their stories. Enjoy!

Questions

Troy writes of his own learning experience while training a horse in the round pen:

> Here I was working to teach my equine partner a simple
> lesson of trust, and I found myself face to face with the
> realization that this lesson was for me. Like a hammer blow
> to the heart, I was reminded of the promises of Jesus:
> - "I will never leave you or forsake you."
> - "I will call you My own."
> - "Seek first the kingdom of God."
>
> The Lord was saying to me, "Troy, you run in circles all
> around Me. Every day you try to do it your way. You get all
> lathered up, sweaty, and exhausted in your day-to-day life,
> not realizing that life begins at My side. Not unlike you with
> Eclipse, I give you the unfettered ability to choose life at My
> side...or not!"
>
> In the embrace of that simple lesson, the Lord of all
> gently reminded me, "Troy, My son, peace, joy, contentment,
> and safety can only be found at My side."

1. Do you find it hard to trust God? Explain why or why not.

2. Share some personal stories about either choosing to trust God or not trust Him. What was the outcome of each situation?

Consider these words from *Average Joe*:

> Life is hard. I get that. It seems as though around every
> corner there waits one more unexpected bill, one more job
> challenge, one more argument with our spouse. And,
> candidly, that's the small stuff. What about our very life?
> What about our eternal destination? Jesus said, "I am the
> way, the truth, and the life. No one can come to the Father
> except through me" (John 14:6).

3. We don't want to needlessly embarrass anyone, but this is
   important. Is there anyone in this group who is not sure that
   he belongs to Christ and is not certain of his eternal destination? If you are that man, now would be a good time to ask
   a brother to pray with you and welcome Christ into your
   heart.

Remember this conclusion from *Average Joe*:

> While His Word certainly speaks of mercy, joy, and peace—
> a life in service to Him—flying close to the Rock can be
> dodgy, challenging, and even dangerous. The Word of God
> is quite clear that, by following Christ, we may lose friends,
> comfort, family, even our life. However, a life sold out for
> Jesus is the very best life we can live.

4. Has anyone in the group faced persecution for being a
   follower of Christ? Share some of these stories.

Troy writes:

> We must get close to Him. Once we choose to embrace the
> calling God has for us, we can do *nothing* outside the
> strength and power of Jesus Christ. The apostle Paul wrote a
> timeless verse in his passionate letter of joy to the Philippians:
> "For I can do everything with the help of Christ who gives
> me the strength I need" (4:13)

5. What challenges are you facing in your life now?

6. What can you do to allow Christ to give you the strength to
    face those challenges?

Consider one more message from *Average Joe*. Take these words to
heart as you seek encouragement and courage to make needed
changes.

> If your life seems boring, uneventful, without purpose,
> I challenge you to take a chance. Fly that little puddle-
> jumper you call "existence" a little closer to the Rock
> that is Jesus Christ.

7. Now that this study is concluding, as you look to the future,
    what are some ways you want to move "a little closer to the
    Rock that is Jesus Christ"?

The TRUTH

> The LORD is my rock, my fortress, and my savior; my God
> is my rock, in whom I find protection. (Psalm 18:2)

Prayer

Take time to let each man share what is on his heart and to be
prayed for. Expect God to hear your prayers and work powerfully in
them.

ABOUT THE AUTHOR

TROY MEEDER is the cofounder and CEO of Crystal Peaks Youth Ranch. From humble beginnings, Crystal Peaks is now a global force in its ministry to children, families, and equine rescue. Married for over thirty years, Troy and Kim have been on *Focus on the Family, Family Talk,* and *CBS Good Morning* and are recipients of the Jacqueline Kennedy Onassis Award for public service. They both speak at conferences, churches, and events throughout America. Troy is an avid fly fisherman, climber, horseman, scuba diver, marksman, and student pilot.

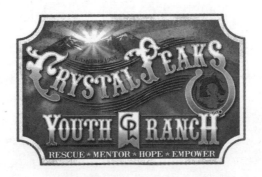

OUR MISSION

Crystal Peaks Youth Ranch was founded in 1995 by Troy and Kim Meeder.

After the rescue of its first two abused horses, something wonderful and unexpected happened; children began to come to the ranch. In their simple but passionate efforts to help the horses, they themselves embraced emotional healing. By what can only be attributed to the compassion of a loving God, the lives of the children and horses began to change.

Since the inception of the Ranch, abuse, loneliness and sorrow have been replaced with peace, belonging and joy. It is a healthy, faith-based environment where children, families and horses choose to embrace hope within the healing circle of unconditional love and support.

Crystal Peaks Youth Ranch exists to
RESCUE the horse,
MENTOR the child,
offer HOPE for the family
and EMPOWER the ministry.

Please visit our website to:

- Learn about our programs
- Sign up to participate in information clinics
- Find similar ministries in your area
- Find out how you can share hope

www.crystalpeaksyouthranch.org

We would be happy to hear from you.
E-mail us at averagejoe@cpyr.org.